Intimacy
Idiot

ISAAC OLIVER

Scribner

New York   London   Toronto   Sydney   New Delhi

Scribner
An Imprint of Simon & Schuster, Inc.
1230 Avenue of the Americas
New York, NY 10020

First Scribner hardcover edition June 2015

SCRIBNER and design are registered trademarks of The Gale Group, Inc., used
under license by Simon & Schuster, Inc., the publisher of this work.

For information about special discounts for bulk purchases, please contact Simon
& Schuster Special Sales at 1-866-506-1949 or business@simonandschuster.com.

The Simon & Schuster Speakers Bureau can bring authors to your live event. For
more information or to book an event, contact the Simon & Schuster Speakers
Bureau at 1-866-248-3049 or visit our website at www.simonspeakers.com.

Interior design by Jill Putorti

Manufactured in the United States of America

10   9   8   7   6   5   4   3   2   1

Library of Congress Control Number: 2014038829

ISBN 978-1-4767-4666-1
ISBN 978-1-4767-4668-5 (ebook)

Some names and identifying characteristics have been changed.

For my mother and father

Contents

- - - - - - -

Intimacy
Idiot

Online Dating Profile

- - - - - - -

Gender
Male

Height
5' 9"

Ethnicity
Tilda Swinton Caucasian

Body Type
Old Lady, Slouchy, or "It'll Do"

Last Online
N/A—this presupposes that there are times when I am *not* online

The first thing people notice about me
If I play my cards right, nothing

Diet
Dairy and its consequences

Religion
Chris Pine

Sign
Scorpio, Nausea Rising

Education
The Hard Way, summa cum laude

Occupation
Narcissism, full-time unpaid internship

Turn-ons
Chest hair, indifference

Turn-offs
Affection, purpose

Exercise
Panic attacks

Have Kids
No, only Chipotle babies

Want Kids
Quiet ones

I am most passionate about
Dinner plans

I spend a lot of time thinking about
When I can sit next

Something no one knows about me
If you have a shirtless picture on Facebook, I've jerked off to it

Four things my friends say I am
Hungry, impatient, neurotic, and, why, what have you heard them say?

My typical Friday night
Wine in mouth, dick in hand, hope in heart

I'm really good at
Sleeping, worrying, busying myself between the thighs of men who have little to no regard for me, eating, ugly-crying to late-career Joni Mitchell, self-sabotage, being at home

I'm really bad at
Cooking, banking, respecting my therapist's boundaries, small talk, big talk, public displays of affection, movies that seem like "work" to watch, quitting while I'm ahead

My ideal day
I wake up in a room that's rapidly filling with Pringles and in order to survive I must eat my way out

Three things for which I am most thankful
Company, a dictionary, Tina Fey

You should message me if
You enjoy moods and trust levels that shift without warning and board games

How I Didn't Learn to Drive

After using his little emergency wheel to pull the car over from the side of the road I was driving on—the *wrong* one—my instructor sat back in his seat, rotated his clipboard in four clockwise angles, and, once my sobs had quieted, very measuredly said, "You know, there are some people who just *don't* drive."

I can just imagine him going home that day and saying to his wife, "I told a student not to drive today, Ruth," collapsing into heaving sobs, choking out, "I'm a man who teaches. I thought I could teach anyone, but—oh, god, Ruth, I *can't*," while she, with her back to him, lets her pots boil over and stares out the window at the line of woods along their property, longing to run into it and never come back.

How I wish he'd pushed me to try again, to try harder, because if you're in the business of making metaphors, my not being able to get myself anywhere is pretty rich. But at the time, it felt like divine intervention. I made eye contact with him for the first time since the driving school parking lot, before he'd become what might in some states be considered my hostage. "Really?" I asked.

"Sure," he said. "You said you want to live in New York, right?"

I didn't get into New York University, and I bet they are *really kicking themselves* now, but I did get into Sarah Lawrence, which was only forty minutes north of the city. I spent my freshman year bouncing back and forth on the Metro-North between Manhattan and the dorm room I shared with two straight guys and the ghost of a Lawrence family servant.

I'd spend weekends in the city, visiting my friends who did get into NYU. We'd wait in line for discount Broadway tickets, eat in shitty chain restaurants because we didn't know any better, and just walk around, because there's nothing better than walking in New York. A friend and I were wandering aimlessly near her dorm above Washington Square Park, and I suggested that we go to the top of the World Trade Center. "You can always go up in that," she said. The next week it was gone.

I still felt too much like a visitor, like the city's houseguest, so the following summer I transferred to Fordham, a Jesuit university right next to Lincoln Center that would only every now and then have a pro-life rally out front. Cramming my hippy-dippy Sarah Lawrence credits into Fordham's very square core curriculum was a hilarious task shouldered by my bone-dry admissions counselor. "What was the name of that class again?" she asked, her fingers hovering above her keyboard.

" 'The Civil War: A Crisis in Gender,' " I repeated meekly.

She shook her head. "Let's call that history," she said, and hit the return key.

On my first night as a real New York resident I cried in bed. Earlier that day, my parents and brother had helped move my friend Melanie and me into our very first apartment, in a Brooklyn neighborhood called Windsor Terrace, with a super who dealt drugs and a homeless man who regularly went through our garbage and tried to sell it back to us. This area was terrorized a few summers ago by a man who kept sneaking up to unassuming women, groping them, and running off. Neither of us was groped when we lived there, but as they say, you can't grope the willing.

Lying there that first night, I thought of my parents and brother in the car on their way back to Baltimore and felt alone and scared. Much like when I sat in the driver's seat and put my foot on the gas pedal and felt the car lurch forward, a murderous mechanical mass, I, too, in that bed felt my life lurching forward, picking up speed.

Suddenly I heard a rapid thumping against my bedroom wall from our next-door neighbor's apartment—his bed. My neighbor, whom we quickly nicknamed The Jackhammer, was less making love to his girlfriend and more belaboring a point. I listened for quite some time, appalled and comforted by it, until I heard his girlfriend shout, "Slow the fuck down!"

For the first time that day, I laughed. I stopped crying and I laughed.

*   *   *

The city hazed me quickly. On one of my first mornings a woman ran into Starbucks and shouted, "Scram, you fucking losers!"

"You in line for the phone?" a man asked me in front of a bodega on Varick Street.

I shook my head no and stepped away from the payphone.

He put a quarter in and dialed. "You fuckin' proud of yourself?" he said. "Don't you fuck with me, kid. You think I won't break into your place and start a fire? You ready to watch every single thing you love fucking burn?"

He hung up and turned back to me.

"Thanks," he said, and walked off.

In my second week, during a sweltering August, the woman standing across from me on the subway lifted her sundress, squatted, and pooped right on the floor of the train car.

On Forty-Second Street, I watched a beat cop break up a fight between a tourist and a sidewalk portrait artist. As I passed them I heard the cop say to the tourist, "Let me get this straight: you thought he was going to draw you *exactly* how you look?"

One morning on the long ride into Manhattan, a deranged homeless man paced the car, threatening a young woman standing by the doors.

"Someone should beat the shit out of you," he said. "Someone should bash your face in. Someone should push you onto the tracks."

Everyone on the train was listening intently, monitoring him, but she didn't seem alarmed. She just ignored him and looked out the window. And then he said, "I'll do it. I'll beat you up." He charged forward and stopped in front of her. "If no one else is gonna do it, I will. I'll knock you the fuck out," he growled. "I'll kill you." She continued to gaze out the window at the dark subway tunnel.

The train pulled into the East Broadway stop. She turned and looked directly at him. "Well," she said, "this is our stop."

He froze, just as startled as the rest of us.

"No?" she asked, and then tossed out a dismissive laugh and stepped off the train.

Coming home late from a movie one night, I watched a small child in a stroller start tossing the balloon he held at the people around him. At first people handed it back to him, but then he'd toss it at someone else, and finally someone tapped the balloon toward the person across from them. The boy squealed in delight and clapped his hands. An older man didn't catch on quick enough, and the balloon landed at his feet. The boy's face dropped. The older man leaned forward—an act no longer easy for him—picked up the balloon, and tapped it gently through the air to me. Again the boy clapped and squealed. For two full stops everybody on that train bounced a balloon back and forth, tasked with not letting it hit the floor. When the boy's stop came and his parents wheeled him out, he waved, leaving the balloon for us to remember him by.

In terms of theatrics and mind-boggling intimacies, the subway cannot be beat—people you see every day and smile at, people who subtly protect each other just by shifting how they're standing, people who compliment each other's outfits, ask where they bought them and for how much. I've seen people meet-cute, make out, and break up. The day Michael Jackson died, a guy played "Man in the Mirror" on his phone and everybody sang along. I watched a woman unzip her jeans so her boyfriend could more easily finger her while their baby slept in its stroller next to them. A breakdancer accidentally kicked me. I've seen ventriloquists, mariachi bands, kid comics, sad clowns, and a guy dressed as a horse who juggled. I've seen people projectile vomit onto the doors and seats across from them. I've never seen a dick, but god knows I see enough of those at home.

The first date I went on in New York was with a film studies major at NYU. We had enchiladas and syrupy margaritas and went back to my apartment, where, after twenty minutes of probably iffy oral, he said to me, "I'm not going to come because I'm on antidepressants, so just, like, whenever you feel done is fine." I didn't know what to do, so I just started blowing him again and tried to count out what felt like a meaningful amount of time—maybe four or five additional minutes—and then, as if his dick was a book I was reading before bed, I just put it down.

"Good night," he said, and rolled over and fell asleep. I lay there staring at his back, flabbergasted. Our passionless encounter hadn't given me any false hope, but I was still shocked by the even less passionate sleeping arrangement.

In the morning we rode the train into Manhattan together. It was a long ride, and about ten minutes in we ran out of things to talk about. After another ten minutes of awkward silence I stood up and told him, "This is my stop," said good-bye, and got off.

It wasn't my stop, and I was late for work as a result, but as I stood in that station and waited for the next train, I felt liberated. He didn't know where I worked; he didn't know it wasn't my stop—I was unknown, and therefore unencumbered. The train with him on it disappeared into the subway tunnel like the city's tongue swallowing him up. I would probably never see him again, but there were several million more where he came from.

It wasn't until after college that I started hooking up with strangers. The AOL chat rooms of my youth went extinct, replaced by sites like Manhunt, Gay.com, and, these days, mobile apps like Grindr, Scruff, and Tinder. You can upload pictures, describe what you're into and what you're looking for, and, in the very New York model of being able to get anything anywhere at any time, basically window-shop for sex from the comfort of your own home. You can swipe and click through profile after profile as if the men were down comforters. Gone are the head- and heartaches, in theory. If someone's not interested, they simply don't respond—there's no chilly brush-off at a bar, no dull, drawn-out dinner. If someone *is* interested, they can be at your apartment within the hour and gone within the next.

The inaugural mate I squired through Manhunt was a graduate student who lived around the corner and, after a couple of messages back and forth, ran right over. It felt like a dream, two hazy but insistent ids conspiring in the night. We stood in the middle of my bedroom, pressed our foreheads together, and tugged at each other until we came. It didn't feel particularly good, and I fretted over how to properly handle a penis other than my own, but after he left I realized it didn't matter if I'd given him a shitty, bush-league hand job—I'd never see him again.

I set out to steady my grip. There was a married lawyer who swung by on his drive home to Connecticut, a Broadway understudy under whom I studied for a night, a junior firefighter who wanted to be peed on, put out like one of his fires. A violinist criticized the paint job in my hallway. A copy editor's shoulders, sunburned from Chicago Gay Pride, peeled onto my face. A graphic designer hugged me hard and cracked my back and whispered in my ear, "I'm one of *those* guys in a relationship. If you see me in public, pretend not to know me."

There's nothing quite like exchanging a polite nod on the street with someone who's been inside you. Many were the mornings I'd see someone I'd knelt before a few nights prior, and we'd look right at each other and not say a word. What was there to say to each other in the daylight, freshly showered and holding iced coffees and on our way to our jobs, at the helm of twenty-four new hours in which we could behave better, be our best selves? No, we'd talk again when the hours waned.

The sex was fairly rote, but the moments on either side of it crackled with glimpses of who these men really were, as if in the scramble to fill the awkward silence they accidentally filled it with the truth. "Text me when you get home or I'll worry," said a guy I'd just blown who refused to kiss me. A stagehand, new to the union and same-sex experiences, rambled nervously about some property he had just bought in New Jersey and the resulting debt. An Italian college student, born and raised in the neighborhood and now raised in my bedroom, complained to me about having to go to Italy for a relative's wedding and how he feared not living up to his family's expectations. I sat up and talked about theater for two hours with a shy set designer who had, earlier in the evening, unzipped his pants and erected a stage you could do *Medea* on.

An individual-giving manager at a nonprofit, after managing to give individually to my nonprofit, kicked back and opened his arms to me. I crawled into them. "What's your sign?" he asked.

"Scorpio."

"Ah. Moody people, Scorpios."

"Sex addicts, too," I added.

"Really?"

"Apparently. Every time I try to get into astrology I open up a book to the Scorpio chapter and it's like, 'You're a jealous, petty sex monster.'"

"Oops."

"Yes, well, my addiction is coupled with an intense fear of intimacy, so . . ."

"So basically you're kind of fucked-up," he said.

"Basically." I covered my face. "Oh my god, why am I telling you this?"

He shrugged. "When I first moved to the city, I was going through a rough patch and was sitting on a park bench crying, and this woman who was also crying came and sat next to me. She told me all about how she was barren and how her husband was infertile and all they wanted was a child. And then she thanked me and said she only told me that because she knew she'd never see me again, and then walked away."

"Oh my god," I said. "That's really intense."

"Yeah."

We stared at the ceiling.

"I should probably get going," he said.

"All right," I agreed.

After a particularly enjoyable hook-up, I asked a short and scrappy medical student if he'd like to spend the night. "Sure," he said. He went into the bathroom to wash his face and brush his teeth with his finger and some toothpaste, and I listened from my bed, thrilled by the sounds another man could make in my bathroom. He faced me as he slept, and I lay awake, marveling at him in the dark. I'd lean in, kiss his collarbone, and quickly lean back, lean in again, smell his shoulder, lean back again, lean in, and bite his hip. He'd stir and groan a little, and finally rolled over to face the other way—my god, the guy was in medical school, he hardly ever slept, and there I was, hey-neighboring random parts of his body all night. In the morning he was distant, and I never heard from him again. It quickly became clear that I'd crossed a line, violated an unspoken set of terms and conditions.

I continued to go on formal dates here and there, but they never thrilled me the way my nightlife did. Still, the idea of a relationship loomed tall ahead of me, an acknowledged destination, but I thought, *Hey, you can always go up in that.*

Subway Diary

- - - - - - -

L train, 1:00 a.m., Friday

I t's the wee small hours, and we're packed in like sardines. Everybody's a little drunk, everybody's a little cranky, everybody's a little horny. I have a coveted standing spot right by the doors, but at Sixth Avenue two gay guys squeeze in on either side of me and continue their conversation with my face right between theirs.

"You can catch it that way?" the taller one asks.

"Oh yeah," the shorter one says, "it's a contact transfer."

"Oh, god."

"What?"

"Uh . . . *I* have it," the taller one mumbles.

I shift in my spot, the best seat in the house.

The shorter one's jaw drops. "What? You *do*?"

"Yeah, I went to the doctor a few months ago and they told me I had it."

"So *I* have it now."

"You do?"

"*Yes!*" the shorter one shouts. "Oh my god. I wish you'd told me this that night in the tent!"

F train, 9:30 p.m., Wednesday

A crazy guy paces the car and sings, "God made! Adam & Eve! Not! Adam & Steve!" and I think, you know, singing that line instead of shouting it, like, opting to give that line melody, is pretty much one of the gayest things you can do.

A train, 7:00 p.m., Thursday

Two guys across from me are complaining about their boss.

"Dude, she is always on my case," the louder one says. "After me about my time card, about the way I answer the phone, always about some shit. I turn around and she's there. She told me to cut my hair. I told her she was jealous that my hair was nicer than hers. She just walked out. She hates me, man."

"Nah, nah, bro," his friend replies, "I think she likes you."

"Likes me?"

The friend makes a sweeping motion with his hand, as if to reveal a diagram of supporting evidence. "She's a bitch to you, she's always on your back. Why else would she be doing all that? She wants you."

After a moment, the louder one says, "I don't know if I could do that whole work-relationship thing, dude. That's messy." Another thoughtful moment. "Although, I guess it's fine if we work together at the beginning, because eventually she'd be home, you know, being my wife."

"Whoa," his friend cautions. "Cart before the horse, dude."

The loud one laughs, and together they watch a young woman's ass get off the train at 145th Street.

The Dolphin from Dubai

He was an Australian flight attendant in town from Dubai, and he only had until dawn. In the doorway of my bedroom he asked, "Are you going to make my last night in New York one to remember?"

"*Yes*," I replied, about as enthusiastically as anyone could, having just been thrust into the Lea Michele subplot of an ensemble romantic comedy.

We'd met online twenty minutes earlier. His face, a shiny new square in the patchwork quilt of familiar faces and torsos, stood out, and even though he was undoubtedly being inundated with come-hithers from my latitudinal compatriots, I threw my hat into the ring. His profile, you see, described a tall, pale foreign tourist with elastic vowels, a clean bill of health, and a fetish for outie belly buttons. Sensing an in, I wrote to him, "I have one."

He wrote back immediately, "No way."

I responded, simply, "Way."

Fun fact: being born was such hard work for me, so arduous, so toilsome, that I emerged screaming with an umbilical hernia that gifted me for life with an outie belly button. I never touch

it; I think it's dark-sided. But, with a man in sight, I was suddenly the old-timey director throwing open the homely understudy's dressing-room door: "You're on tonight, kid! Learn the
steps from Daisy and keep those lips *closed when you smile*."

"Send a pic?" he requested.

Obliging, I lifted my shirt and began to wildly photograph
my stomach. I applied a tasteful Instagram filter to the best shot
and sent it off. He responded with a slew of exclamation marks
and slobbering emoticons and begged to be invited over. Turns
out my milkshake can bring *one* boy to the yard: a fetishist.

He sat on my bed and he didn't slobber, he didn't mouth-
breathe, he didn't writhe—what did he do? He grinned sheepishly and said, "Sorry, I'm a bit shy." He was awfully cute. I sat
down next to him. "How old are you?" he asked.

"Twenty-nine," I replied.

His mouth dropped. "No way," he said. "I thought you were
my age."

He told me he was twenty-three. "I'm not that much older
than you," I started, but he cut me off with, "No, it's just—you
look good, you look young."

"Well, you know," I replied. "Advances in medicine."

He told me my cardigan was lovely, and, as though someone had pressed play on a Paula Cole song, I jumped on him,
koalaed myself to his body, and put my mouth on his. He was
a fantastic, tender kisser, and his hands were deft and assured,
strong, I could only assume, from maneuvering the beverage cart
up and down countless airborne aisles. He lifted my shirt and
kissed his way down to my belly button, where he hovered rever-
ently. I squirmed.

"Sorry, it's just—" he said, and brought his mouth in for a landing. I sat up instantly, and he pulled back. "Is that okay?" he asked. "Is that weird?"

"No, no," I replied, wanting to be hospitable. "It's just—new."

He dove back onto it and I flinched.

"Oh, wow, you hate this!" he exclaimed.

"It's just that—no one has ever done anything to me there before," I told him.

"Really? What have the other boys done, just gone around it?"

I didn't want to tell him what the other boys had done, but did offer that, yes, the few who had taken a passing interest in my pleasure had indeed gone around it. He shook his head, staring at my outie with the same love in his eyes that appears in mine when I see passed trays of cheese at a reception. I ran my hands through his hair and told him to go slowly, which he did. He kissed it gently once, and then several times more. It was the most personal impersonal thing I've ever experienced. My body filled with emotion, as though I might at any moment cry or laugh or poop, so I put my hands to my face and quickly chose laughter.

The truth is, I'm scared of my belly button. My childhood doctor told me that I should never travel anywhere that was more than an hour away from a hospital because my intestinal wall could rupture further and I'd start to, you know, come out of myself, unspool. This was summarily debunked years later by my uncle, who's also a doctor. But I've tiptoed around my weird navel ever since, as though it held the key to my mortality, and now I'd, what, invited someone over to put his mouth on it and potentially suck the life out of me.

"Okay, I think I'm ready to move on to other things," the Australian said. "Sorry, I'm a little fucked-up about sex. Not many things turn me on, outside of my fantasy life."

"Oh yes, yes," I murmured, steamrolling over *that* little tidbit and kissing him again. I wanted to busy his mouth, lest he tell me more about his fantasy life and disrupt mine, in which he was someone who knew me and loved me.

It worked.

After we finished, he put his arm around me. It was one of the first warm nights of summer, and we lay in the breeze from the fan in my window. He didn't much want to talk about living in Dubai. This was his first visit to New York, and while he'd ascended all of the recommended tall buildings and waited in line for all of the recommended pizza, he'd mainly come here to wander, to get lost, to walk the streets and follow their concrete whims.

"I want to be a town planner," he said, "and I'm *mad* for your grid."

He'd spent the previous afternoon wandering in disoriented circles through the West Village, and as he told me about it his eyes, like towns themselves, lit up. He'd be back as soon as he could, he said, but the New York flights were the ones all the flight attendants fought over, and he didn't have much seniority yet. "Plus I'm taking two weeks off to go to Berlin for a convention," he added. "Not for work, though." I asked him what for. "One of my passions."

"Oh, is it a town planning convention?" I asked.

"No, my *other* passion."

"What's your other passion?"

He looked at the ceiling and sighed. "This is where you ask me to leave."

Oh, god, I thought, *the aforementioned fantasy life and Berlin.* "What's your other passion?" I asked again, picturing a bunch of neo-Nazis doing bath salts in an Embassy Suites.

"You didn't notice anything out of the ordinary in my picture?" he asked.

That's when his profile picture flashed back to me: him sitting on a carpet, smiling, wearing normal clothes, being hugged from behind by someone in a full fox costume. *Full fox.* Again I sat up: "Oh my god, are you a furry?"

He nodded sheepishly, and the word "sheepishly" suddenly had a different luster.

"You are?" I asked again.

"Yes," he said. "You didn't guess that from my picture?"

I'd thought he was at a theme park!

A furry, for the uninitiated, is a person who identifies very deeply with, and dresses up as, an anthropomorphized animal. There have been quite a few evening news segments devoted to them, with lots of ominous music playing over shots of Care Bears walking down the street holding hands. YouTube it.

"Do you want me to leave?" he asked.

I laid a hand on his chest. "No, but I will need you to answer some questions."

How long had he been a furry? "Since I was eighteen, but I'd had inklings earlier." Who was the fox in the photo? "My ex." Was he also a fox? "No, I'm a dolphin."

"But dolphins don't have fur!" I said, and he rolled his eyes.

"They don't need to *literally* be furry," he said. "It's whatever animal you are on the inside, whatever you identify with the most. Me, I've always felt like a dolphin, because I'm happy and thoughtful and, like, really alert and intuitive."

"So you have a dolphin suit," I said.

"Yes."

"Do you have sex in it?" I asked, and again he bristled.

"No—it's too hot, and the suit gets sweaty," he replied. "Also, it's a *very small* subset of furries for whom it's a fuck thing. For the rest of us it's not. It's about play, it's about affection, it's about snuggling and tickling and wrestling. Frolicking."

"Frolicking," I repeated.

"Yes."

"Frolicking where?"

"Anywhere. In houses, or outside—fields, parks. There's a frolic in Central Park tomorrow, actually, that I'm going to be missing because I leave—"

I cut him off: "I'm sorry—there's, like, an organized, formal frolic?" He nodded. "What does everybody do?"

"Play. Skip. Roll around."

"In broad daylight."

"Yes. You get a lot of kids wanting their picture taken with you. It's harmless and fun."

I asked him if he'd brought his dolphin suit with him. He shook his head. "It doesn't travel well." He looked at my clock. "I need to get going soon. They lock the doors at two o'clock."

"Who's 'they'?" I asked, and saw him pause, weighing honesty's worth, before answering.

"I'm staying in a furry house nearby."

My eyes grew wide. "A furry *house*—you are not—you are

not staying in a furry house!" I gasped, and slapped at his arm. "*What is a furry house?!* Is it in a tree? Is it just, like, a grassy knoll with a door in it?"

"It's an *apartment*," he replied. "A four-bedroom apartment. I can't tell you where it is, but it's in your neighborhood."

You guys: four furries live there—one's a DJ, one's a painter; one's gay, two are straight, the fourth is "other"; they take in traveling furries, everybody sleeps on bunk beds—I know what you're thinking: somebody throw TV money at this. He said it was okay with them that he hadn't brought his dolphin suit. "They have a trunk of things you can wear while you're there."

"And do they have sex in the costumes?" I asked, now just taking notes for pitch meetings.

"That's not the point," he said. "It's about being fucking quiet together and being soft and being fucking close to one another, without all the talking, all the games, all the human bullshit. Do bears fuck all the time? No, they just hold each other for an entire season."

"That does sound nice," I found myself saying. I didn't really know what else to say—certainly not anything about the *other* things bears do. My mind raced. "So your ex was a fox?"

"Actually, my last three boyfriends have been foxes."

"Agile hunters," I offered.

"Fuck you," he replied.

I ran a hand down his body and asked, "So do you feel like you're slumming it with me? I'm no fox."

"No—it's nice, it's refreshing. But it's frowned upon; I can't really tell other furries about you."

That's too bad, I wanted to say as I watched him dress,

because I'm going to tell everybody about you. He turned back to me, almost as if he'd heard me say it, and as he did I tried to imagine a smiling, hairy-chested bottlenose buttoning his shirt at the foot of my bed. What I saw instead was someone remarkably self-possessed, someone who knew exactly who he was, fully aware that it might get him asked to leave. I admired that; I've begun to have trouble even admitting what I'm looking for to a salesperson in a store. I was aroused anew, and I asked him to stay.

"Can't," he said. "But the next time I can get on a flight to New York, I'm yours."

He kissed me and then his lover, my belly button, good-bye. I thought it'd be appropriately swoony and cinematic for him to let himself out, but he had trouble with the door and I had to go help him—it really is a bad knob.

It's been a while since I swam with the Dolphin, since my night in the Cove, but I continue to think about him. I mean, people have forged lives together despite weirder kinks. I'd much rather my husband be squirting water out of his blowhole in the pool than jerking off with a belt around his neck in the garage. My therapist assures me that I'm not a latent furry, but I don't know, if being a furry means cuddling and being fucking quiet together, I can get on board, at least on birthdays and harvest moons. I wouldn't be a dolphin, and I wouldn't be a fox; I would without question be one of those squawking birds that are always freaking out in a tree.

I was out to dinner with two friends who are a couple, and I asked them what animals they would be. One, who later revealed he thinks of himself as a wolf, turned to the other and said,

"What animal do you think I'd be?" and his boyfriend replied, "Oh, I think you'd be just the cutest little piggy." A chill hit the table, and I'm pretty sure they fought when they got home.

I'm imagining our wedding, the Dolphin's and mine: half old New York, half Noah's Ark. Big dinners with all of our friends, some around the table, others at the trough, bottles of wine and buckets of chum always within arm's reach.

I'd still want to raise the children human, though. For holidays.

Cooking for One

- *Easy Coq au Vin* -

4 teaspoons all-purpose flour

4 bacon slices, finely chopped

4 skinless, boneless chicken breasts

3 tablespoons fresh Italian parsley

8 ounces large crimini mushrooms, halved

1 ½ cups dry red wine

3 texts to him, unanswered

1 ½ cups more dry red wine

1 additional text, slightly burned

1 feeling, sinking

2–4 tears, to taste

People's Parties

Some people are great at parties—they know exactly when to arrive, how much to drink, and, most importantly, when to leave. Me, I've arrived so early I've had to devein shrimp, I've laughed wet bursts of wine onto people's faces, I've tucked hosts into bed at evening's end.

Here's my usual party strategy: find the liquor, find the food, find the space where two walls meet. Alienate enough people around you to have some breathing room. Find the attractive people—this shouldn't take long; they'll be the ones getting everything they want in life. Once you've found them, stare hungrily at them all evening, and interpret every alarmed flicker of eye contact from them as a new stage in your relationship.

If an attractive person comes over and says something to you, perhaps something like, "What are you doing over here in the corner?" always, *always* look behind you, because nine times out of ten a fellow attractive person has strayed from the pack and gotten lost, like a glamorous lamb with a fade and Macklemore tickets, and is merely being retrieved.

If the attractive person is indeed talking to you and seems interested, genuine, or even flirtatious, you're probably going to get murdered. You could do worse; an ax in the back is still penetration. Is he smiling, laughing, touching your arm, telling you you're funny? Yeah, you're going in a well. He's going to make a coat of your skin. But the joke's on him, because you've got eczema.

I was in the kitchen at a friend's holiday party, hiding near the people I knew and the champagne punch I'd just met, when I caught sight of a good-looking young man sampling cocktail wieners from a Crock-Pot on the counter. I'd had half of a pot cookie and two cups of punch, so I felt emboldened enough to lean in and ask him, "How are those wieners?"

Unfortunately I wasn't emboldened enough to ask this in a flirtatious tone, so I sounded like I was conducting a door-to-door survey for Crock-Pot.

"Good," he replied, spearing three wieners on a toothpick.

Still not quite nailing a flirtatious tone, still sounding like someone's inquisitive niece, I asked, "You take three at a time?"

"Yup," he said, popping them into his mouth, adding, "I'm a triple threat."

I laughed congenially, trying to imagine the shadow his jaw might cast in the glow from my Christmas tree. Pleased, he reached across four people to tap his friend on the shoulder and say, "This guy asked me if I was taking three at a time, and I said, 'Yeah, I'm a triple threat.'"

They both laughed loudly.

He turned back to me. "I dare you to take four," he said.

Before I could think better of it I popped the wieners into

my mouth, where they promptly exploded with hot, wet salt. I covered my lips daintily and looked to the floor, as if he might still find me demure even after I'd housed four cocktail wieners in one bite, like a python who just wants to belong.

When I looked up his friend had joined him. They were angled toward each other in a bitchy migratory *V*, watching me make not-quick-enough work of a mouth full of spiced meat. His friend leaned in and whispered something in his ear, and they both laughed. It was like middle school; it was like they were bullies in the fucking gay schoolyard, where the sandbox is full of cheap coke and the slide is shaped like a raised eyebrow.

Later in the evening I stood in the corner of the living room with my mouth full of cheese cubes and my eyes full of the hostess's best friend, a lawyer. Gay, Prince Eric–handsome, and super solvent. I inched my way toward him, desperately racking my brain for legal jargon, when someone seized the hostess's iPod and put on "And I Am Telling You I'm Not Going" from *Dreamgirls*. I saw this as a clear in. I turned to the lawyer and said, "Oh my god, did you hear her mother was just murdered?"

Without skipping a beat he turned to me and calmly said, "This isn't Jennifer Hudson. This is Jennifer Holliday. The original?"

Apparently his field was musical-theater crime.

I slunk away and took a seat off to the side. That's when George, an uninvited neighbor who'd spent all evening going around telling each female in attendance that they looked like a porcelain doll, plopped down next to me. "Are you gay?" he asked.

"Yes," I said, wondering if George knew how long I'd waited for someone to compare me to a porcelain doll.

"Hey, that's cool," he continued. "I love gay people. I'm not gay. I'm into chicks. That's my thing, what can I say."

"Yeah," I said.

"Hey, man, you've actually got an advantage over me. Girls automatically like you because you're gay, and then you can bone them."

"Well, there's a flaw in your plan," I said, "because I want to bone guys."

He leaned in. "Listen, I'm going to tell you something," he said, suddenly serious. "Don't ever let anyone tell you that there's something wrong with you. You hear me? You are just like the rest of us. We're all human beings. Some of us like chicks, some of us like dudes." He put a hand on my shoulder. "You—you are normal. There is nothing weird about you. You hear me?"

"Yes," I said.

"You don't have to hide."

"I'm not, I just told you I was ga—"

"Don't feel on the outside, looking at us. You're inside, you're in with us, you're just like us at the end of the day, you know?" He leaned his head against the wall behind us, then turned to face me. "I'm a motivational speaker. And I want you to hear what I'm saying."

"I do; I'm feeling quite motivated."

"Look, you'll do fine. If I was gay, I'd probably take you out."

"Well. Maybe in another life."

"Yeah," he said, closing his eyes. "See you there."

Love Poem for the Guy across from Me on the Subway This Morning

———————

When you withdrew an apple from your bag
I thought, *Oh, god, it's gonna get loud up in here*,
but
no,
you chewed with your mouth closed
the entire time
and even dabbed at your lips with a napkin
to catch any excess juice that might have escaped,
but none did—
escape was only hypothetical
because your subway table manners were exquisite
and those lips never parted midmastication.

The serpent successfully offered Eve a bite of an apple
from the Tree of Knowledge,
and should you offer
a similar bite my way
you will be met with similar success.

I could be the Eve to your serpent—
a nearsighted Eve with irregular sleep patterns
that result in increased emotional fragility,
but an Eve nonetheless,
an Eve who wants to Know things,
wants to Know what it's like to be Known
by a genteel young man
in a colorful button-down
who abides by the food pyramid.

Poser

Early Signs

I was the last person to realize I was gay, and even that didn't take very long.

My coming out went pretty much like this:

ISAAC: I'm gay.

MY MOTHER & FATHER: We know.

And:

ISAAC: I'm gay.
MY ENTIRE HIGH SCHOOL: Um, we know.

And:

ISAAC: (*sobbing at a bonfire*) I'm gay!
MY SLEEPAWAY BIBLE CAMP: (*making lanyard crosses*)
We know. *God.*

This is not to say that I have never experienced homophobia in my life, but in my coming out there were no slurs hurled, no tears on the banister, no fainting spells. There was only a mild level of resentment for implying my friends and family were deaf, dumb, and blind.

Even Santa knew:

When I was in the first grade, my teacher called my mother. "Isaac is running around slapping all of the other boys' bottoms," she said.

My mother—after, I imagine, an internal sigh—asked, "Are the other boys complaining?"

"Well, no," my teacher continued, "but I just thought you should know."

"Why don't you call me back when there's an actual problem," my mother suggested.

I mean, everybody had a lot of time to grapple with the fact. Case in point, before I was out of diapers I was in sensible pumps and shopping for toiletries:

Everywhere I went I'd swap shoes with the girls:

Whenever I could get my hands on some Barbies I would. I devoured animated movies and storybooks. *Cinderella* was notably my jam, until I was introduced to live action, and by live action I mean Julie Andrews. I spun around on my parents' bed in my mother's dresses, playing Maria in *The Sound of Music*, and meticulously re-created the scene from *Mary Poppins* in which Mary summons a great wind to blow away the other nannies lined up outside the Banks household. Here I am, a prospective nanny in line for an interview:

And, oh! Here's the wind:

You may think this pose is accidental, the bend and angle of each leg, the arching of each foot; it was not. I held it until we got the right shot.

I turned the couch into a royal bed of pillows and blankets and laid in artful repose on it, Sleeping Beauty asleep in her castle. I turned two box fans on high, draped blue bedsheets over them so they'd thrash like a churning sea, and, as Wendy, walked the sofa arm plank. And from the same thrashing bedsheet ocean I'd emerge, a Little Mermaid longing to be where the people are. Never once did it occur to me to play the prince; that unfortunate task fell to my younger brother, who I hope can someday forgive me.

Catwoman Arrives

When previews began airing on television for Tim Burton's *Batman Returns*, I was transfixed by Michelle Pfeiffer as Catwoman and began purring and prowling around the house. In the alley behind our duplex in downtown Baltimore I wrote, directed, produced, and starred in a roller-skate extravaganza called *Batman vs. Catwoman: On Skates!* I enlisted all the neighborhood children and cast them accordingly. There were actual girls on hand to play Catwoman, but none of them had the intrinsic feline quality I was looking for, so they were relegated to mere concerned citizens of Gotham. Only one actress was up to the task:

We made posters and popcorn. All of the kids' parents emerged from their houses and set up lawn chairs along either side of the alley, and you know what? They watched all of it, an eight-year-old boy rolling around meowing in his mother's slip, and at the end of it they clapped, folded up their lawn chairs, and went back into their houses. God bless them.

An urgent trip to Toys R Us begat a Catwoman backpack

(which I wore to school for most of fifth grade), a Catwoman poster for my bedroom wall, and a Catwoman costume, which I wore to school on Halloween:

Here are two Batman scenes I wrote when I was eight:

Penguin and Chocolate-Chip Cookies

BATMAN: Hey! How did the cookie jar get empty again?
PENGUIN: I can't help it! It's not my fault. (Exit Batman.) Chocolate-chip cookies follow me everywhere I go. (A cookie drops out of his shirt as the curtain closes.)

Catwoman Goes to College

CATWOMAN: College starts inn [*sic*] 4 more years. When I'm in college, I want to be the prettiest and smartest girl in the whole class.

PENGUIN: Want is a good breakfast, but it is a bad supper.
CATWOMAN: When we go to college, Penguin, I'm not
going to room with you.

Hollywood Murders

My head filled with narratives, cinematic and epic, and I began
to write them down—"Hocus Pocus at the Hospital," "Murder
at Midnight II" (there was no "Murder at Midnight I"), "Death
Becomes Miss Scarlet," and "Dear Diary, It's Me, Lois Lane."

A sample from "The Hollywood Murder," age nine:

> *I arrived at the birthday party for Marilyn Monroe. I, Sarah Jessica Parker, accompanied by my friend, Geena Davis, didn't know what we were doing here. We saw Madonna drinking Cokes.*
>
> *"I hear she's coming on stage in fifteen minutes," said Madonna.*
>
> *"That's wrong. Twenty minutes." Marilyn Monroe stepped out of the shadows. I looked away in disgust. I couldn't bear to look at the dresses she wears. Too short. Yuck!*
>
> *Nicole Kidman and Tom Cruise walked in. "Hello," Nicole Kidman said. Tom Cruise was staring at our host. I pointed to Nicole. She took one glance at her husband. She stepped on his toe.*
>
> *"Ow!" he yelped.*
>
> *"Just remember I'm your wife," she said.*

My stories took a hard right toward *The Pelican Brief* after
that. My mother started giving me her John Grisham novels
when she finished them, and eventually I outpaced her and
started checking them out of the library myself. The stories I
wrote were ludicrous.

Here are a couple of snippets from "The Richland Murders":

Melissa opened the desk drawer and saw it was empty.

"I haven't quite moved in all of my appliances for journalism yet," Tracey answered.

"I see. Well, you are new to Richland, huh?"

"Yes, I'm from Idaho. A small house around Twin Falls. My boyfriend and I moved here. Except Paul's in Seattle with Lily."

"Who's Paul and who's Lily?"

"Oh, my daughter is Lily, and my boyfriend is Paul."

"How can you have a daughter and no husband, just a boyfriend? You had a child before you were married?"

"No! Lily's thirteen and her father died on the coast. Naval officer. Boy, I miss him."

Melissa nodded and said, "Have you heard any good gossip lately? All I've heard is that Dana and Michael Bucksteen were smuggling cocaine to the Mafia."

And later (I know you're on the edge of your seat):

"Timothy Jones, Richland Police Department. Found a couple identified as Dana and Michael Bucksteen dead in the river. Found their Mercedes, too. Nice-looking car, before the deaths. We think they died either of suicide or murder. If it was murder, we think it was because they worked at the Richland Post." He covered his mouth suddenly, and then acted as if he had never said anything about the Richland Post. "No, just forget what I said. We were talking about the deaths, right?"

"Do you think it was suicide?" Tracey asked.

"Probably. Either that or it's murder."

And who could forget this nail-biter:

Jessica Savors walked up to her house. She was a lawyer, and lived in Shanghai, Japan [Shanghai is in China]. She was Japanese, but spoke perfect English language. She was quite attractive, but still did not show off. With a turn of her key, the door opened. The smells of sushi went up her nose. Her husband, Brian, sat watching the baseball game.

"Hi, Brian," she said.

"Hi, Jess," he said.

They kissed, and she walked over to the oven and pulled out the tray of sushi. Just where she'd left it.

Merely a page later:

"Brian, believe me. This is very hard to say. Do you remember that time when my brother was shot in the park when I was taking a walk with him?"

"Of course I remember that. It was very tragic."

"What I'm saying is that I killed my brother!" Jessica cried.

"Why would you shoot your own brother?"

"I don't know, I don't know," Jessica said, clutching her hair. "He . . . he got drunk with his friends in the bar. I didn't want him driving home, so I walked him home. He was so drunk, he turned on me and attacked me. That's when I pulled out the gun and shot out of shock and defense."

Poor Jessica Savors.

Beach Babe

Here I am, in my mother's bathing suit, giving you more face than advisable for my age:

I'll have you know I art-directed this whole picture—the bedsheet is the pure white sand, the sofa cushions are rocks on the shore, and the green rugs propped up on broomsticks are palm trees.

It is not lost on me that behind each of these shots is a set of parents who held the camera. If they were concerned or weirded out, they didn't let it show. I was, and am, very lucky. Maybe they wanted to see how it would play out. They probably thought they had a budding drag queen on their hands, but honestly, I think it was less the gender and the clothes that appealed to me and more the thing that occurred last to me: that these women, these Disney damsels, were pursued and loved by men. Also, and this is perhaps even more key, that they didn't have to do anything for it. In most cases all they had to do was sleep.

Subway Diary

A train, 11:30 a.m., Tuesday

"What've you been up to?" the man across from me asks his friend, a former coworker.

"I got a tattoo," she says.

"Nice!"

"Not nice. Listen to this. This shit only happens to me," she grumbles. "It's misspelled."

"What is?"

"My tattoo."

"It is not."

"It *is*," she moans. "I said to Crash, I said, 'Did we or did we *not* run that through the spell check?' and he was like, '*Uhhh*, I thought we did.' It's horrible."

"Can I see it?"

"Nah, it's around my boobs."

"You gonna get it fixed?"

She sighs. "I'm going in next week and the guy's gonna see what he can do. But what's he going to be able to do, you know? It's words."

"Sorry, I don't mean to laugh."

"No, laugh, go right ahead. Crash was like, 'Who cares? It'll only be me seeing it,' and I said, 'Well, get your fuckin' laughs in now, 'cause I don't want you laughing every time I take my shirt off.'"

"I'm sure it's not that bad."

"I told Crash, I said, 'So what are you saying, you're the only one who's gonna be seeing it? Well, you better fuckin' marry me, then.'"

They laugh.

"So we might get married," she says. "We'll see."

1 train, 10:30 p.m., Thursday
A handful of musicians get on at Lincoln Center and stand above me, midconversation. The cellist is saying, "And after she came out to her parents, it was like, yeah, she's a lesbian, but her parents are, out of nowhere, really prejudiced. So, who truly came out to who, you know?"

"I didn't know who my mother really was until I was sixteen," one of the violinists offers.

The others balk.

"Seriously, I thought my mother was my aunt," she insists. "But it was actually the other way around. This all just accidentally came out at Christmas."

"Awkward Christmas," one of them who plays maybe an oboe, I don't know, I'm guessing by the instrument cases, says.

"Jack Nicholson thought his mother was his sister," the guy holding the double bass pipes in.

"Oh yeah, *Chinatown*," the cellist says.

"No, like, in real life. His mother was really young—like, she had him when she was a teenager, and he grew up being told she was his sister or something."

"God, that's intense."

"Happened to me, too, guys," the violinist interrupts. "My mother was my *aunt*. Hello?"

A train, 2:00 a.m., Saturday

It's dead quiet. Like cosmopolitan krill we sit, carried north by the creaky tide. The man sprawled along three subways seats across from me stirs, sits up, and says to a woman near him, "That looks very nice on you." He gestures to her pashmina. "That looks nice," he repeats.

"Thank you," she says.

"I can say that, right?"

"Sure."

"Those things always make women look nice. I notice things like that," he says. "I look through the magazines and I see what makes a woman look nice." He scratches at his head. "You going home?"

She nods.

"You work in an office?"

"Yep."

"Office jobs'll kill you," he says. "Everybody thinks it's nine to five, all the time, you know, but it's not. It's not everything. There's more to the day. I used to work at the World Trade Center, you know, I'd set up meetings and calls and stuff, and you know what? Things would change. I'd set up everything, and then suddenly the meeting would be cancelled, and it's like, it's not everything, you know? You know?"

"I do."

"I truly think God saved my life. You know why? If I'd still been working there, I'd be dead. But I lost my job, I sucked, they hated me, so they fired me. I think about that all the time; if I'd been better, I would've still been working there. I mean, what the fuck."

She nods, smiles sympathetically.

"Did you lose anybody?" he asks.

"No," she says.

"Thank god," he replies. "Oh, sorry." He picks up the Doritos at his side. "You want some chips?"

"No, thanks." She smiles.

"You have kids?"

She shakes her head.

"Do you want kids?"

She scrunches her face. "Maybe."

"You know what I say? Every woman is a mother, and every man is a father. We all raise kids together. We help out."

"Ha."

"It's true."

"No, that's, that's nice," she says. Suddenly it's her stop. She gets up to leave. "Nice talking to you," she says. "Take care."

"Hey, thanks," he replies, stretching back out. "I'll try."

My Kind of Bar

- - - - - - -

B eing relatively young still, and desirous of external stimuli, and nocturnal by nature, and avoidant of duty and responsibility, I am often out at night. This poses a conundrum, since I am also averse to standing, shouting, and swaying.

It's hard for me. My murse cuts a wide swath, and my glasses fog up. I walk into a bar and look like the first person to be murdered in an Agatha Christie novel.

"Where do you want to go?" friends will ask me.

Where do I want to go? I want to go to a bar that has the following:

Rosé & Oyster Mondays

Ample seating, with murse hooks

Chips & Salsa Tuesdays

Hot stone massages

Zach Quinto Wednesdays

Bartenders who can hear you

Vodka-Soda-Sorrow Thursdays

No PDA, no elbowing, no talk of your web series

Reading Too Far into Old Text Messages Fridays
No dancing, sit down and listen to the lyrics
Jane Campion & Cardigan Weather Saturdays
A side room where you can Facebook everyone in the main room
Egg Buffet & News Bloopers Sundays
Late Night Sunday Foam* Party

Meet you all there.

---

* Memory Foam.

Zoo Stories

- - - - - - -

I work in a box office. I sell theater tickets to people. I'm not a Chilean miner, but it's customer service and shit can get real.

"It must be really boring to work in there all day," a little boy said to me as his mother signed her credit card receipt.

"Ferdinand!" his mother exclaimed. (I'm not embellishing, his name was Ferdinand; white people are the worst.) "It is very rude to make fun of someone's job," she scolded. "Say you're sorry."

"It's okay," I started to interject.

"*No*," she snapped, my feelings no longer her concern. "Ferdinand, say you're sorry," and Ferdinand did, and Ferdinand learned a big lesson that day, and Ferdinand will be a walk in the park for future lovers.

It's been eleven years—eleven years of sitting alone in a box reading articles about how sitting kills people. Eleven years of smiling through bulletproof glass as people let their soft-serve melt all over the windowsill. Eleven years of answering the same two questions: "What's the running time?" and "Where's the restroom?" (Roughly translated: How long do I have to stay, and where can I shit?)

In my sophomore year of college, I responded to a posting for a part-time box office job at a nonprofit theater in Times Square. I didn't have any box office experience, but I'd been a hostess at a Red Robin, a balloon inflator and ribbon curler at a Factory Card Outlet, and a sales associate at the Scholastic Store, where I rang up *Harry Potter* books, wiped sticky child palm prints from every flat surface, and helped Kirsten Dunst pick out a face-painting book—not for a child, but for her and Jake Gyllenhaal.

I got the job.

If you're wondering where all your town's assholes are, they're in Times Square. A few years ago they paved over large sections of Broadway to make the area more "pedestrian-friendly," which has only made Times Square feel like some sort of pre-Rapture tailgate party. To get anywhere, you have to maul your way through throngs of horrible people just standing and staring up, waiting not for some ethereal force but to see themselves in the Forever 21 jumbotron. I quickly learned how to maneuver through the neighborhood with as little street time possible. Each day I scurry like a rat through hotel lobbies, parking garages, and, once, a *Law and Order* shoot to get from the subway to work to Chipotle to work to the subway again.

The box office itself is a small rectangular space, large enough for two people to sit in it and read about Tilda Swinton's throuple all day. Everything is gray: the carpet, the walls, the desks, and, at the end of the day, your skin. The desk chairs are ergonomic, which means you get a good stretch in every time a wheel comes off or an armrest slips out. There are a hundred network cables tangled on the floor like spaghetti, and you have to be sure one isn't looped around your shoe or you'll unplug the entire operation. A floor-to-ceiling window looks out onto a rock-and-trash

Zen garden full of smooth pebbles and candy bar wrappers, receipts, Playbills, and empty Starbucks cups that were blown one story up from the street by the wind.

The majority of my interactions with customers go something like this:

ISAAC: Hello, how are—
CUSTOMER: Two for Thursday.
ISAAC: —okay.

The two customer groups with whom I interact the most are Wall Street Dicks, so pissed they have to sit through theater to get laid:

WALL STREET DICK: I don't know, wherever, as long as she can see. You got a bar here, chief?

and Ancient New York Broads:

ANCIENT NEW YORK BROAD: Can you guarantee me that I can hear from this seat? I go to the theater five nights a week: Stockard Channing, speak *up*.

These women—I love and fear these women—these women are museum pieces, they are Fabergé eggs frowning on a cross-town bus. They love theater, but fuck you if they're going to act like it. They lower their Chanel sunglasses and look at a seating chart as if they're preparing for battle—which, according to them, they are, with giants: "The last time I was here, li-ter-ally, a *giant* sat right in front of me. Couldn't. See. A *thing*. Thank god I know how *Hamlet* ends!"

They travel in packs, like the velociraptors from *Jurassic Park*, feasting not on children but on discount codes.

"Do you have a discount code?" one asked me.

"Do *you* have a discount code?" I replied.

"No. Do *you?*"

They could do this all day.

"I don't provide you with the discount codes, ma'am," I said.

"But don't you put out the discount codes?"

"When they are being offered, yes."

"So can't you just give me one?"

"No, discount codes have to be discovered by the patron."

She tapped her fingernails on my windowsill and leaned forward. "So there *is* a discount code."

"I didn't say there was a discount code."

"Have people brought discount codes in to you today?"

"I will not answer that question."

She threw up her hands. "What did I ever do to you?"

I kept my eyes trained on hers and tried to not show fear.

Finally, with a huff, she tossed her gold American Express onto my windowsill. "You know," she said, "the last time I asked for a code at the box office, the lady just gave me a discount. She just gave me a discount, no trouble at all. That was at the Mint Theater. A *serious* theater, the Mint."

Every Saturday matinee the River Styx ferry docks at our theater.

"Is there an intermission?" a sweet, grandmotherly type asked on her way into the theater.

"Yes," I replied.

"Fuck!" she shouted. "I hate intermissions!"

They're hooligans. I've had graying tongues stuck out at me. Arthritic middle fingers have endeavored upward in my direction. "How do you sleep at night, charging so much for theater?" another hissed. "The Greeks did it for free!" She wore a loose sweater and no bra, and when she bent over to pick up her bag, suddenly there it was: a witch's tit.

Another got off the elevator in our lobby and just started shouting at the top of her lungs, "HELLO? IS ANYBODY HERE? HELLO?" When she got to my window, she flung out an arm and exclaimed, "There you are! Didn't you hear me calling to you?"

I did, I wanted to say, *but I am not paid enough to call back to you. This is not the woods. We did not just survive a plane crash.*

Other notable customer groups include Drunk Guys:

DRUNK GUY: Three tickets for the seven thirty—sorry, am I talking really loud? I'm kind of drunk.

Wise Guys:

WISE GUY: You can sell me a student ticket; I'm a student of life!

and Girls on Their Phones:

GIRL ON HER PHONE: Two tickets under Johnson.

ISAAC: First name Sara?

GIRL ON HER PHONE: Yes, ma'am. (*looking up*) Oh, sorry. Sir.

People will press their foreheads right up against the glass. "Whoa, it's like you're in a zoo," they'll say. I've wiped spit, snot, and soda from the window. People openly burp. A man clipped his thumbnail while waiting for me to print out his tickets. A woman ran from the bathroom to the theater entrance, pulling up her jeans and zipping her fly, fastening her belt. She bowed before the door usher so he could see the ticket clenched tightly between her teeth.

"Are you ready for us?" a colorful older man asked.

"We're very organized," his equally colorful wife interjected.

"Don't put your hand on his window," he told her.

"He's my social secretary," she said to me. "I go wherever he tells me."

"That's nice!" I said. "I'm jealous."

"Don't be," she replied. "We're retired now. We see nothing but theater and each other."

"First things first," a woman said to me. "I want you to know that it is easier to get into *heaven* than it is to get a ticket from your box office."

"All right," I replied. "I'll pass that feedback along."

*   *   *

"Do you have any tickets to *Obama*?" a man asked me.

"Do you mean *Othello*?" I asked.

"Oh, yeah," he said. "*Othello*."

You can tell everything you need to know about a person by the way they treat someone in a service position. If you're on a date with someone and they're rude to the waiter, shut it down. I mean, blow them first, because nothing beats a hand on your head from someone with a chip on their shoulder, but shut it down after. Consider: Is this someone who allows for a scenario in which they might be at fault? No? Bid that party an Irish good-bye.

"I *never* would have clicked the matinee instead of the evening!" is something that is shouted at me on a regular basis.

"It happens," I say. "The buttons are small and close together—"

"No, your website screwed up—I *never* would have chosen the wrong performance. This is your *website's* fault," the customer will insist, and I can see in their spouse's eyes a pleading look of *Just agree with him, just say it was the website, what do you care, you're not the one going on another wilderness immersion with him this summer.*

Many husbands won't let their wives talk, even if their wives ordered the tickets.

"Tickets under Rose Fletcher," the husband will have no qualms announcing, his wife just a meek set of bangs on tiptoes behind his shoulder.

"I need Rose's signature here for the pickup," I'll say, sliding a pen and a receipt through the slot toward the bangs, and he will take the pen and sign her name.

"I just got the strangest feeling coming in here," a woman said, stepping breathlessly to my box office window.

I looked up from my computer game. "You did?" I asked.

"Yes; not a good feeling," she replied, her eyes darting around the lobby. "Like things are, *whoo*, not okay here."

I paused. "What do you—?"

She cut me off. "I'll be quick: Could I get four tickets for Friday?"

"Can I call you directly for tickets?" a man asked. "I don't want to speak to someone in another country or whatnot."

"You can't call me, but anyone in our phone room can help—" I started.

"Isn't *that* a phone?" he asked, pointing toward my desk.

"This?" I asked, lifting what he was pointing at.

"Um, *yeah, buddy*," he snarled.

"This is a calculator."

"Do you have a single ticket available?" an elderly man asked me.

"No, we're sold out, I'm sorry," I replied.

"There's something disappointing about you," he said. "You make everybody sad."

*   *   *

Some favorite customer names: Aaron Kuntz, Barbara Lillycrapp, Daisy Poon, Artemis Goldberg, Ben Aufill, and Heidi Ho.

"And how did you hear about the show?" I asked an older woman.

"My very first boyfriend gave me a book of Shakespeare's sonnets that I loved," she answered. "So when I heard there was a show with the sonnets I knew I had to come. I invited him, but he's married now, with children. Grandchildren, too."

"Oh, I'm sorry," I said.

She shrugged. "That's the course of true love, some sixty years later. The French had the right idea. Marriage, with lovers." She looked at me. "Oh, never mind."

"Our tickets are in the front row," a man said, "but we just had a big, heavy meal and we're both worried we might fall asleep. Do you have anything farther back?"

"I don't, no; we're completely sold out. But who knows, maybe you'll enjoy the play enough that you'll stay awake!" I replied.

"I don't know," he said. "We are so full of pasta."

"What's got better seats, April or May?" an elderly woman asked.

"May's better by far," I said.

"Fine, let's look there," she replied. "Hopefully we'll still be alive then. Do you do refunds?"

*   *   *

Once, an older man hobbled up to the doors of the theater hold-ing out his ticket, which was sopping wet. "It fell into the toilet," he said with a grin. "I want to see if it'll still scan."

"Sir, we'll reprint your ticket for you," I called out. "You can throw that out."

The ushers tried to point him to the nearby trash can. "Nah, I want to give it to this chickie here," he said, hobbling over to the box office and offering it to my coworker Cristina, who simply turned away from him. He dropped it onto my window-sill. "Better use tweezers to pick that up!" he said. "Better get a diphtheria shot!"

A man soiled himself in the lobby and refused to leave, per-haps eager for the authentic Elizabethan experience of watch-ing a three-hour Shakespeare play while sitting in his own shit. Three-quarters of the way through an unflinching British rela-tionship drama staged in the round with full fluorescent lighting, a woman lifted her prairie skirt and peed into her empty conces-sions cup. The actors could, no joke, hear pee filling a plastic cup in the middle of their scene. She left it there after the show. An unwitting usher, thinking it was maybe our house chardonnay, approached her after the show, saying, "Ma'am? I think you left your cup." She whipped around and screamed in his face, "It was your fault! You trapped us in there! I had no other choice!"

"Is this production modern dress?" a young woman asked.

"I *loathe* modern dress," her mother added archly.

"Mother, please," the daughter said. "You've endured modern dress before."

"It was Stratford-upon-Avon, and even then the only thing keeping me in that theater was that it was Dickie Burton. We don't go to the theater often, but when we do, we do it *right*."

"Mother, stop it, or I'll have to punish you," the daughter threatened.

"Go right ahead. Hit me in my stomach," the mother countered. "It's too big anyway."

"Hi there, I'm calling with some good news about your tickets for Thursday!" I said on the phone to a customer.

"Good news is bad news in a tie," he replied.

"It's an architect's city now," an older woman commented, apropos of nothing.

"What do you mean?" I asked her.

"It used to be for the people," she continued. "At Juilliard, there are all of these stairs now up to the front entrance. The security guard told me the students have to take a side elevator. A *side elevator* for the double basses at Juilliard. I'm only saying this because it's all over the city. It's a blight. There's a stairway to nowhere in front of the symphony. And everything's glass now, smooth glass. There's nothing to hold on to when the wind blows."

She smiled.

"You're busy, you're working," she said.

She blew me a kiss.

"Nice talking to you," she added, walking off.

Songs customers have walked up and caught me singing along to: "Diamonds Are Forever," "This Kiss," "Landslide," "Nessun Dorma."

"I'm hoping I can switch your seats ever so slightly to accommodate a patron with mobility issues," I said to a woman with tickets in the front row.

"I don't know," the woman responded. "I'm extremely sensitive to perfumes and fragrances and I spend most shows with my face buried in scarves." She wrung her hands together. "Okay, fine. Who are you moving me next to? Can it not be a woman?"

"Hey," a middle-aged man said with a grin. "If Sharon Stone comes up looking for a ticket, seat her next to me, will you?"

"I'll do my best," I said with a laugh.

He laughed as well, and added, "I used to work in a mail room, and there was a guy I worked with who'd always toss the letters at the slot. They never made it in, but he'd say, 'At least people see me trying.'"

Divorces are awkward. "Oh, it looks like you might be in our system already," I said to one woman in the midst of a sale. "Are you still on East Seventy-Third Street?"

"I was when I was married," she replied. "So let's update that. And my last name, too, if you don't mind."

Once, a man called in a fury. "My wife and I *just* separated, and we had tickets to your show that *I* bought, but she has them in her possession," he fumed. "If she tries to use them, please do not let her in. She is not authorized to use them. I didn't buy them for her to use without me, so, please. Do not let her in."

One Valentine's Day, I couldn't find a woman's tickets. "Is there any other name they could be under?" I asked.

"No," she snapped, turning to her husband, muttering, "I can't believe this. He can't find the tickets."

When I swiped her credit card, an entirely different name came up in the system. "Could they be under 'Morris'?" I asked.

"Oh, yes," she said quickly. "Morris, that's my maiden name—I used my maiden name, I forgot." She turned to her husband. "Sorry," she said.

"Well, Happy Valentine's Day," he quipped.

"I'm looking for two tickets to *Jew*," a hammy middle-aged woman declared.

"*The Jew of Malta*?" I asked, for clarity's sake, and also because, come on.

"My husband and I met doing a production of it," she added. "We've been married for twenty years now. We're both actors, you see. I've been on all the *Star Trek*s, and some of the bigger-name actors are absolutely awful." She clasped her hands together. "Not the star of *your* production, though, I'm sure."

"No, he's very nice," I said.

"My husband, in *Jew*, did a deadfall where he just fell and hit the stage in the Riverside Church and the place shook. People thought he was dead. That's how good he was," she said. "Now he's disabled. Too many falls."

"I want to look like the dancers in this show, they're so thin," a woman said to me. "I really hope I didn't offend this fat lady at the bus stop today. I was talking about how fat I am, and she looked at me like I was crazy. I don't look too bad, do I?"

"No, not at all," I said.

"You don't want to hurt my feelings," she added. "I've been crying enough today."

"What's your name?" a woman asked me.

"Isaac," I told her.

"Oh," she scoffed, "like in that Bible story I hate. God tells Abraham to kill his only son, Isaac, and Abraham is about to, to prove his love, as if love needs to be *proven*, I mean, when has anything been proved to *us*, and then God's like, 'I'm just kidding.' I heard that story when I was five years old, and I knew then and there that I hated God."

A little while ago, I handed a pair of tickets to an attractive young straight couple. "Yikes," the young woman said to her boyfriend, reaching for the tickets. "This guy has worked here a *long* time."

Eleven years minus vacation time, sick days, and "sick days" equals roughly 528 weeks. Forty hours each of those weeks means 21,120 total hours, or 880 days. Basically, I could enroll my cumulative time in this job at Dalton.

Fuck.

Coming Up

- - - - - - -

I'm in the passenger seat of a BMW that's tearing up the West Side Highway. The driver is a young corporate guy I met on OkCupid who lives in Westchester but comes into the city several times a week. We're coming from a bar that was so loud I just kept nodding and smiling, completely unable to hear anything he was saying, but now that we're in the car I like what I hear. He's a little caustic because he works with money and not people, but he's got a worldview and he's funny. Also, his arms flex impressively while gripping the steering wheel, and I think of all my jars that need opening and all my fears that need assuaging, and it is clear to me that I cannot let this guy go back to Westchester tonight.

We reach my street at the top of Manhattan, and he pulls over in front of my building. He puts his hazards on. I do not heed their blinking intention. Keep in mind: I've been watching a lot of *Sex and the City* lately, on which everybody is always inviting someone to "come up" after a date. I think to myself, *Be like on the TV.*

"How do I get back to the highway from here?" he asks.

"You just keep going straight down the hill, and then you make a left at the light. There'll be signs," I reply, trying to give off a few of my own. "But . . ."

"Cool." He drums the steering wheel. "Well, this was nice."

"Um," I say, "do you want to, maybe, come *up* for a bit?"

"No, sorry, I should get back to Westchester—"

"THAT'S OKAY! THAT'S OKAY!" My voice leaps two octaves, I'm shrieking, his windows nearly crack. "THANKS-FOREVERYTHING! DRIVESAFELY!"

I unbuckle my seat belt and fumble with the passenger door handle. Because his car is German and punishing, the automated seat belt strap wraps around my neck and pulls my head toward the dashboard. He has to help untangle me, his arms flexing for me one last time. "You got it? Here, don't *struggle*, just let it— reach for the . . . loop it—okay, you good?"

Needless to say, my e-mail the next morning is unanswered. The seat belt and I, however, go on to have a couple of nice dinners.

A Few Key Erotic Moments
from My Early Adolescence

- - - - - - -

The third step was always the tattletale. It would creak under the weight of my tiptoed foot, as if calling out to my sleeping parents, "*Creak,* not for nothing, but your gay son is sneaking down to the basement to do god knows what!" I learned quickly to avoid it on my descent.

As a teenager I snuck two floors down to the basement on an almost-nightly basis to poke around on the Internet, instant-message with friends, and jerk myself senseless. A stack of weathered inkjet-printed pictures under my bed had served me nobly up until then—Marky Mark grabbing his Calvined crotch, Brad Renfro crawling shirtless down a hallway, and Jared Leto leaning toward the camera in an undershirt, thumbs through his belt loops, arms slightly flexed, and eyes slightly glazed (my god, I'd kill to be able to feel something now from a picture of *arms*)— but I was craving more: I was craving images that moved.

Throughout the day and early evening I'd keep a tape in the VCR, and whenever so much as a sleeve rolled up on whatever I was watching, I hit record. Then, when the rest of the house was peacefully slumbering and I'd made it safely to the basement, I'd review the day's catch: James Marsden shoveling manure shirtless on *Second Noah*, Dean Cain answering the phone in a towel on *Lois & Clark*, Thomas Calabro rolling around with Laura Leighton on *Melrose Place*. If nothing struck my fancy—and my fancy was easily struck; I once jerked off to Rodgers & Hammerstein's *South Pacific*—I made do with what we already had in the house. You know how some people can just whip up a dinner with whatever's left in the fridge? That's like me and jerking off. In the family VHS collection, there was Kevin Costner in bed with Amy Madigan in *Field of Dreams*, Disney's gay-porn Brendan Fraser vehicle *George of the Jungle*, and the copy of *54* I'd somehow convinced my parents to buy me (no small feat, seeing as how they were not as easily fooled as my friend Nicole's mother, who let us rent *Boogie Nights* because we told her it was about the Holocaust).

In my book, Ryan Phillippe gets his own paragraph. Do you remember where you were when you first saw his face? I do. It was at a Halloween party in 1997, and we were all half watching *I Know What You Did Last Summer*. He appeared on the screen like a cherub-curled, cobblestone-stomached miracle. It was like when someone sees Jesus in a piece of toast. *Cruel Intentions*, a veritable candy store for this sweet-toothed kid, featured his butt in the shower, his chest in the bed, and his fingers in the Vampire Slayer. And in *54*, which is basically a ninety-minute ogle, I lived vicariously over and over again through Sela Ward—so wonderful on *Once and Again*, whose love scenes with Billy Campbell from that show often wound up on my daily clip tape—as she ran her hands up and down his torso. Ryan Phillippe, pouty-lipped patron saint, justified and fortified my gayness. It was like, *Oh*, that's *what I do it for. That's why I put in the long hours.*

*   *   *

My best friend from elementary and early middle school taught
me how to jerk off. He's essentially the reason I don't write more.

I was over at his house one afternoon after school. His parents were both tenured at a local college and never home. On
their massive computer screen he brought up a topless picture
of Jenny McCarthy and eagerly turned to me for a reaction. I
was already certain that Jenny McCarthy and her ilk just weren't
going to take, thanks to a few key erotic moments from my early
adolescence:

(1) I read my father's childhood anthology of *The Hardy
Boys* and felt a thrill other than that of the case.

(2) There was a brawny-tawny college-aged counselor at
my sleepaway bible camp who was sporty, affable, and hugely
evangelical. If scripture was going to be read, I wanted to hear
it from him. We'd barely spoken all week—he'd taken more
to the rowdier boys in my cabin, the ones who were always
wolfing down dinner so they could get back outside and toss
a Frisbee around—but on our final night, while getting into a
pose for a group photo, he grabbed me and hoisted me onto
his shoulders. "Hey, man, get up here," he said. "Up we go."
His Frisbee-calloused hands were warm on my knees, steady-
ing me. I, afraid to touch any part of him, clenched my fists
and rested my forearm on the top of his head. He was probably just trying to imagine the weight of a cross on his back,
but no matter. In the photo my smile is huge, and my eyes are
two saucers—matching, of course.

(3) Sully from *Dr. Quinn, Medicine Woman*.

(4) My grandparents took my brother and me on a road trip to Mesa Verde one summer. They gave us each a disposable camera. My brother took a few halfhearted but entirely appropriate pictures of the ancient cliff dwellings. I took a ton, but in the foreground of all of them is a boy around my age in an ill-fitting Denver Broncos Super Bowl Champions T-shirt with a flawless curtain of blond hair falling over each ear, his dark eyes hanging in boredom from having to go look at a bunch of dumb rocks, *god*. I can only imagine my grandparents' bewilderment when they leafed through the developed photos and saw the blond boy talking to his mother in the middle of an intricate stone bath, the blond boy scratching his ear in front of what used to be reservoirs, the blond boy directly above me, ascending the thirty-two-foot ladder to the highest cliff dwelling, his Broncos T-shirt stuffed into the back pocket of his shorts and his bare back glistening in the Colorado sun, a shot I must've taken one-handed midclimb.

(5) During orientation on the first day of sixth grade, the boy standing next to me turned and, out of nowhere, said, "Might be time for a haircut." Crushed, I had no response; I just stared blankly at the single chest hair right below his clavicle, exposed by the unbuttoned polo he wore that day and all the days after. I soon learned his clavicle looked best in the waning fifth-period light. I loved him. He was so mean.

"Have you ever masturbated?" my best friend asked, Jenny McCarthy's ample bosom still in front of us.

I shook my head. "No, never," I said.

"It's fun, it feels really good," he replied. "Do you mind?" He unzipped his khakis, pulled out his dick, and slowly began to demonstrate. It felt impolite to not in turn pull out mine, so I did, and tried to replicate his movements. We didn't say a word, he an angular science nerd and I a coarse-haired theater wisp, but he was assured and authoritative, a gentle guide who led by example—an impression currently shared by his students on Rate My Professor.

We jerked off together all the time after that. We'd drop backpacks and trousers on opposing sides of whoever's room we were supposed to be studying in, settle, and silently busy ourselves, or we'd sit parallel in his parents' desk chairs, watching porn or a sex scene from a movie on their computer. We never touched. Internally I had fully acknowledged my desires—down with the Catwoman poster, up with Jonathan Taylor Thomas's *Got Milk?* ad—but it never occurred to me to make use of the other dick in the room. It was always about what we were watching together, what was on the screen. We were merely separate drivers caravanning toward the same destination.

Maybe a year or so later I told him I was gay. We were walking by a creek, because, like I said, I wanted my coming out to be as dramatic as possible. "I could say one of three things," he replied. "That I'm okay with it, that I'm not okay with it, or that I'm gay, too, and in love with you."

I laughed and was like, *No, really, can we talk about me some more?* and that was that—and, you know, it's not until now, years later, as I'm sitting here writing this paragraph, that I realize he was probably being serious and going out on a huge limb with me in that moment. The thought that he could've cared for me in that way, or desired me in that way, never even crossed my mind—with Chris O'Donnell on our screen, what on earth could he want from *me*?

He had a thick Polish dick, real smarts, and, now, a PhD and a wife. I don't blame him for ignoring my friend request.

I began to wade into the murky water of AOL chat rooms. Quickly I tired of the gay rooms and headed for the straight ones. Within a matter of minutes I'd made a fake female profile and was instant-messaging straight guys.

"a/s/l?" they'd ask.

"16/f/portland," I'd reply.

"I'm in Portland too," one guy wrote back.

"maine/oregon?" I asked.

"Oregon," he replied.

"i'm in maine," I responded. "☹"

My name was always either Becky or Jessica. I wasn't into frivolous girly stuff; I wasn't a cheerleader, I didn't like animals, or Britney Spears. I much preferred my studies and Lauryn Hill and going online and grilling guys for exhaustive details about their dicks. You know, like every teenage girl. God knows the guys with whom I was cybering probably weren't sixteen, either—they were probably fifty-four—and we were just sending stock photos culled from our Altavista searches back and forth. But the anonymity was thrilling. I felt confident, suddenly able to articulate the things I was too nervous to say out loud to someone in person.

*   *   *

I left my diary open on my bed one afternoon, an action my father insists was a subconscious plea for their involvement, and I'd say he was probably right. When he went in to turn off a light I'd left on he read the first entry he saw, an unnamed free-form piece that I will now title *Without A Doubt I'm Gay (All the Ways I'd Blow Brad Renfro)*. "That's not a respectful way to think about someone, to objectify them in that way," my father said. "Sex is something that happens in a relationship, between two people who love each other."

But I was unstoppable; I was sure there were countless other ways to blow Brad Renfro I hadn't even thought of yet. I jerked off all the time, in the daytime even. I forgot to lock my bedroom door once, and my mother walked in on me with laundry. I brazenly did it in front of the television one afternoon—I don't know, Pacey was, like, wearing a V-neck on *Dawson's Creek* or something, so it was urgent—and down my mother came with more laundry. We were never without clean clothes, I'll say that much.

When my parents started finding traces of porn—random pop-ups, typing in "H" and having the search engine recall a search for "hairy hunks," a weathered VHS in my backpack that I'd gotten from a friend at school—we fought. "Sex is about respect!" my father shouted. "This is not respect! This is not love!"

It's still a bit of an issue. My parents read everything I write, and there's a cost to my frankness. My mother once said, "I want you to find someone nice. I want you to stop letting all these guys come on your face and leave!"

If my writing has done anything, it's taught my mother the phrase "come on your face." I'm not proud.

"Stop writing about all this sex!" she continued. "You can

write about things you see around the city, or things that happen to you at the box office . . ."

"You don't want me to try to experience companionship?" I asked.

"Companionship, sure! But you keep writing about seeing people you've had sex with on the subway."

"It's just—part of it," I stammered out.

"I don't see people I've had sex with on the subway," she said.

My father, also on speakerphone, piped in, "That's not true, Meg. You've seen *me* on the subway."

Heeding my parents' distinction, I set out to acquire for myself a loving, respectful situation with a man. I soon learned that, unlike in your imagination with a man on a screen, this requires reciprocation. Like a copy of *The Canterbury Tales*, I went untouched for most of high school, with a few notable exceptions:

On the Knee: A handsome young actor who's now on your televisions put his hand on my knee at the end of a van ride from the Miami airport to the hotel where we would spend the next week as winners of a national high school arts competition and said with exasperation, "You've never heard of Joni Mitchell?"

I've since learned that someone's hand on your knee is a nearly valueless gesture—the penny of PDA—but at the time I appraised it highly. "No," I replied, trying to quickly commit to memory the weight and warmth of his open palm. "What does she sing?"

"*Blue*," he said, removing his hand.

"What?" I asked, devastated at the loss.

"Her album *Blue*. Just get it and you'll understand. It's my favorite CD ever. That CD is me."

He was from Plano, Texas. I thought it was remarkable that such an urbane gay boy could emerge from somewhere as desolate-sounding as Plano, Texas, but since then I've learned that handsome, protean gay actors are Plano's largest export, having met a *billion* of them in New York. But if that CD was him, I wanted to listen to it; I wanted to learn every word. So, back home a week later, I bought *Blue*. It was the beginning of summer. I opened my bedroom windows and lay barefoot on the rug and pressed play. From the CD player fluttered this crystalline voice above the insistent strumming of a single dulcimer: *I am on a lonely road and I am traveling, traveling, traveling.*

I listened to the album over and over again. I loved it. I didn't know what any of it meant, but like someone learning Italian through conversation exchange, I began to learn older, wizened, weathered, wistful. Joni Mitchell begat Carole King, Judy Collins, Bonnie Raitt—music best summed up by my friend who heard me playing it one night and said, "Oh, my mom played this in the car the night we left her second husband."

But that's what I wanted, to be on the other side of love—to have had it, as though heartbreak was chicken pox and you were then immune.

On the Arm: At one point during my senior year, one of my best friends at the time, a short, rakish straight boy, was waiting for me by the doors to the cafeteria on my lunch break. He grabbed me by the arm and pulled me into the boys' locker room, which was empty because we went to an arts high school. He sobbed uncontrollably for a good half hour, choking something out about a mean classmate. She'd called him stupid, and he was far from stupid, but his father had called him stupid a lot when he was younger, and there he was, a boy again, pacing, fists clenched, pounding his thighs. I remember sitting there with him, reeling from seeing him cry, my heart breaking, just so high-school-in-love-with-him.

Again, ours being an arts high school, the parties thrown were less about drugs and alcohol and more about sexual exploration, like Studio 54 but with Matchbox Twenty performing. To kick things off, everybody started basically in a heap on a beanbag, kissing whoever was closest, and eventually separated into duos, trios, quartets—herds, prides—and disappear into other rooms to put things places. I never did; "The Virgin Isaac" was my nickname. I was always upstairs watching *I Love Lucy* with the timid and the overeaters. My rakish straight friend had systematically hooked up with all of my female friends at these parties, and I'd press them for details after. I learned that his tongue was stabby, that his stomach was a rock, that he liked to cuddle. "You have the best blowjob dick," one of my less discreet friends told him in front of me as we all walked to class together the morning after a party. "It's the perfect length."

"Thanks," he said, and then we all, I don't know, talked about Kristin Chenoweth or something.

I found out recently at a gossipy dinner with old friends that he was, at the same time, fooling around regularly with another boy in his class.

Now, he'd confessed to me that he had experimented with boys before, at summer camp, which was apparently what everyone did there. Everyone except for me; I spent my summer camp days weaving in the crafts shed and my summer camp nights fearing the Watermelon Man, an evil, deformed creature that my counselor had seen in the woods. I would sleep over at the rakish boy's house, and he'd sit with an arm around me as we watched TV. I rested my head on his shoulder the entire bus ride back from a day trip to New York. We'd hug hello and good-bye. Whenever I could I'd put my body against his, and he seemed to allow it. I figured that should he ever want to experiment again, I would be the likely candidate, because I was the person he could cry to. Yeah, no. Turns out he got his muscular Jewish rocks off with a blond twink who's now a jewelry designer with a line for dogs.

He stayed with me when he was visiting New York a few years ago, and it was awkward. We were different people, important to each other in the past. The pain I feel is residual, pain for the seventeen-year-old me who longed to be with and under him. Today, I realize the novelty and loveliness of being someone a man can cry to, put his arm around during *Friends*.

Around the Body: As a freshman in high school I fit snugly into the arms of a junior, and I noted this each time we hugged, which wasn't often, but it was often enough for me to listen to Jewel's "Pieces of You" for hours on end and write egregiously bad poetry about him. We were in *Guys and Dolls* together—he a supporting lead and I one of the ~~Hot Box Girls~~ ensemble gamblers. He sang beautifully, was well-liked, and had a warm smile and a big, genuine laugh. Every day I'd think about him, wonder when our paths would cross, agonize over what to say. I knew between which periods we'd pass each other in the hallway, each flanked by female friends. Some days he'd smile and say hi, and I'd ride that sensation through the next few periods. Other days he'd be distracted, not look up, and it was all "Pieces of You" all the time on those days.

One night, nauseated and sweaty-palmed, I called the number on the *Guys and Dolls* cast contact sheet and, when he answered, told him I was gay. "Oh, really?" he replied. "Well, tell me, how are you feeling?" He was probably just being polite, but the fact that his reaction wasn't a *yeah, duh* meant the world to me. We talked for over an hour about his experience coming out, about our families, about school. I was very clearly infatuated with him, and he was very clearly not with me, but he befriended me nonetheless. After school he'd drive me in his mom's cherry-red Mercedes to diners, the mall, and sometimes downtown to the café on Baltimore's unofficial gay block. These were wonderful afternoons—he'd get tea and I had my first sips of coffee, we were out among the adult gay men whose ranks we longed to join, something other than second-divorce music was playing in the background—and then he'd drive me home, duped into chivalry by my not knowing how to drive.

I've gotten rid of a lot of the poetry because it's embarrassing, but I wouldn't trade the countless hours I spent pining on my bed for anything. My romantic imagination developed then and has thrived ever since. I learned how to make something out of nothing. He was the great unrequited love of my young life. He was my coming of age.

We became dear friends, but I continued to hold a torch. He came to visit me in New York when we were both in college, and when he told me about all his debaucheries in acting school I was judgmental and horrified. I felt betrayed, protective of the fantasy he'd tarnished. "I hear all these things about what you're doing at school," I said, "and I'm asking myself if I can still love you."

He leaped to his feet, furious. "That is the most hurtful thing you've ever said to me."

"Well, the answer is always yes, I still can!" I tried to explain.

"What's wrong with you?!"

"I'm still in love with you!" I cried.

He shook his head. "I told you, I don't feel the same way. But I do love you. And I would *never* ask myself if I still could, no matter what you told me," he said, and stormed into the living room to sleep. The next morning he left without a word.

His feelings for me had matured over the years, and mine hadn't. It hit me like a ton of bricks: *That's a person.* You can't hit pause or rewind or fast-forward. You can't put in a different tape.

Throughout my early to mid-twenties I continued the pesky habit of mistaking close friendships with men for untapped romantic scenarios. I would sit down with one friend after another—some of them even *straight*, my god—and confess my love to them. They'd all turn me down very graciously, and our friendships, thankfully, have all survived. Funnily enough, as soon as I told them I had feelings for them, those feelings evaporated within me, and before the sentence was even fully uttered I knew it was no longer true.

What if it's the wanting you want and not the having?

Oh, god.

It's so much easier with someone on a screen, someone made up of blues, reds, and greens, someone conjured by phosphors and fluorescents.

Subway Diary

A train, 8:30 p.m., Wednesday

A mother tries to fend off her newborn daughter's impending tantrum while standing in the middle of the car. Not a single person offers her their seat. A young Asian couple sleeps in a pair of seats across the way. The woman's head rests on the man's shoulder while he has one hand on her waist and the other cupping her jaw (um, sweet?). A father-son duo begin arm-wrestling with such frivolity that I downgrade the older man from father to uncle to youth minister as the match intensifies.

Next to them a young man holds his young daughter as she sleeps. The man across from them suddenly says, "You don't seem nervous that I'm looking at your bag."

The young father gestures to the pink backpack on the floor between his feet and asks, "What, this?"

"Yeah," the man says.

"Okay," the young father responds.

"I've been staring at it."

"You have?"

"You aren't worried I'll steal it?"

The father laughs. "What would you steal? Baby stuff?"

"Right, right," the man says, laughing as well.

"You want some diapers?"

"Nah, nah."

"You want a bottle?"

The man stands up, the next stop his. "You have a good one," he says.

"You, too, man," the father says, shaking his head.

B train, 3:30 p.m., Friday

It must be scientifically impossible for a group of teenage boys to ride the subway together without saying "faggot" thirty times.

There's discord among today's group over the whereabouts of the clitoris. Like generals before an invasion, they each argue their own strategies for search and seizure. The one most sure of its location stands when he speaks—this is when the scene takes on a real *Inherit the Wind* tone—and the others sit rapt, listening to him tell of his first sighting of The Clit, his attempts to bridge their rocky cultural divide, and how The Clit now prefers his diplomatic efforts over all others.

I make eye contact with the woman across from me, and she rolls her eyes and smiles.

A train, 3:00 a.m., Sunday

The man across from me says to his female companion, "You know, there's a part of Long Island—have you heard of Long Island?"

She nods.

"Well, there's a part where it's all Persians."

"Oh, wow," she says, "I'm Persian-Armenian."

"I thought you might be," he says. "You have that air. What's your name?"

"Matilda."

"Oh, I love that name. Do you ever go by Tilda? There's a famous actress named Tilda, you know."

The train pulls into the High Street station.

"Is this my stop?" she asks.

"No, we aren't even in Manhattan yet," he says. "You're so cute, ha. Can't get away from me that fast. Look, we should exchange numbers. I'm not hitting on you or anything, but take my number."

She takes out her phone. "Okay."

"Nine one seven."

"Uh-huh."

He looks over her shoulder. "Nope, you aren't even—you aren't even on the right screen for it. You aren't going to call me; why do I—you won't call—but, at least for the illusion, put my number in." He takes her phone from her and types it in. "There. Now when you delete it you'll at least be deleting my actual number; give me *that* dignity."

She reads from the screen: "Asshole from the subway."

"Saved you the trouble," he says, winking. She laughs. "Call me sometime. I can get us floor seats to pretty much anything—Lady Gaga, Michael Bublé, you name it."

"All right."

"You aren't going to call. You so aren't going to call. It's okay. Look, you can't hurt me," he says, throwing his hands up. "You can't hurt me."

"I am just thinking, maybe you will get back together with your wife," she says.

He shakes his head. "No, no."

She leans in, shoulders him playfully. "No?"

"Her family is very influential."

"So?"

"So, they hated us together. We were dreamers. That's what we did: we dreamed. We were like hippies, kind of, and stupid. That's what she said the last time we talked; she said we'd been stupid and she regretted all of it."

The train pulls into the Chambers Street station.

"Is this my stop?" she asks.

"No, no, you've got a bunch more," he replies. "Go look at that map. Look at it. Manhattan's real big, and we're only at the bottom of it."

Love Poem for the
Tall Drink of Water
Who Shushed the Loud Gay Guys
next to Me at a Concert

– – – – – – –

Oh
my
god
thank you.

They were being so loud,
right?

I'll never understand why people go to concerts just to stand
at the bar
and fucking
talk.

The worst kind of people.

Good heavens, you're tall.

Hi. I'm down here.

At every play, at every movie, at every concert,
every event where someone is performing
and silence would be appreciated
I want you with me,
you respectful redwood,
you polite Paul Bunyan.

I want to climb you like Everest.
I have the upper-body strength
of a prepubescent girl,
but if I know there's a meal at each base camp
I'll muster the will.

You have a gold chain around your neck
that twinkles when light hits it—
is that so planes don't fly into you by accident?

We could traverse the world together,
you and I, shushing loudmouth fuckheads
everywhere we go.
I'd ride your shoulders and slap traffic lights,
pick flowers from second-floor window boxes
to tuck behind your ear.
To your hair I'd give a gentle tug
whenever my curmudgeonly ears caught the sound
of discourteous discussion—
since I'm a WASP I'll genetically sense disruption
before you—
and that's when you can shush them.

Afterward we can go to my apartment
which, while lacking a decent cross breeze,
does have high ceilings
under which you can stand comfortably.

At night I'll sleep hugging your leg
like it's a pillar
on the Parthenon that is your body.

After you've shushed my downstairs neighbors, that is.

Traveling Alone

I don't know why the situation thirty-nine thousand feet above the middle of our country is so fraught. Nebraska's airspace in particular reminds me of several power addicts I've gone to bed with. I can never sleep the night before flying—I'm too worried that I'll miss my flight, that the plane will crash, that the person next to me will have brought food from home. That's why, regardless of my flight time, I'm always at the airport at 3:15 in the morning. And you'd be surprised at how long the security line is at that time.

On a recent trip I was waiting in line and a TSA lady came up to me and asked, "Are you alone?"

My god, is it that obvious? I thought, checking my face for fresh tears, and she clarified, "Are you traveling alone?"

"Yes and *yes*," I replied, and she whisked me off to what I hoped would be a fabulous singles-only line but in actuality was the employee security line. I took my belt and shoes off with the Hudson News ladies and the guy who buffs the floors.

Never travel with me, for I am cursed. My seatmates on every trip appear to be sent by some sort of agency. I once sat next to a girl who continually blew reams of snot into the sleeves of her sweater and folded them up, like quesadillas. One guy kept sending his friends live selfies of his raging sty. A girl wiped her boyfriend's face down with oil blotter sheets and, when he refused to take them to the trash can, placed the used sheets in the seatback pocket.

On that day's flight the girl in the seat next to me brought—you guessed it—Food from Home, a Ziploc baggie full of pretzel bites and a Bosc pear that she chomped and slurped and nibbled at until it was seeds and a stem, and I'm convinced she only stopped there because we'd landed and they turned the lights back on.

Look, Food from Home is the second-worst thing you can bring onto a plane. The list goes:

1. Bomb
2. Food from Home

I've spoken with the FAA about this at length, and we all agreed that I should never call again.

My issue with Food from Home is not the smell, nor is it the sound—it's the sentiment. The thought of someone standing in their kitchen cutting up celery or spreading fucking almond butter on spelt bread, thinking in a sing-songy voice, *Just a li'l snack for the plane!* is excruciating to me. That person is not a team player. That person has broken the unwritten code of travel, in that we've all agreed to be collectively miserable and get through it the best we can. Unless you brought enough hummus for all of us, kindly leave it at home. That's why it's *at* home, because home is better than an airplane.

Once, on a red-eye back to New York, the woman across the aisle from me pumped big globs of sanitizer onto her bare hands and rubbed them all over her seating area, even going so far as to ask the man in the seat next to her to raise his arm so she could "get the armrest." She spread a napkin across her tray table and pulled a full sleeve of saltines and a handful of McDonald's ketchup packets out of her carry-on. She opened the sleeve, squirted a perfect stripe of ketchup from the bottom right to the upper left corner of the saltine, and ate the cracker in one bite. She pulled out a new saltine and ketchup packet and repeated the process, on and on, until the entire sleeve of saltines and pile of ketchup packets were gone. The direction and shape of the ketchup stripe never varied. She folded the ketchup packet carcasses up in her napkin and handed them like a gift to a passing flight attendant.

Next, she opened a box of chocolate-covered macadamia nuts and spun each nut around between her teeth, sucking the chocolate coating off until each was just a naked macadamia in her palm. She bit each macadamia in half and chewed and swallowed one half, then chewed and swallowed the other. In this manner, she finished the box.

Then she had an orange, which, to her credit—I'm not entirely unfeeling—she ate like a normal person.

The majority of my traveling is done by bus. I've tried to find a fraction of delight in being rolled from city to city in a giant Tupperware full of smells and sounds, but I can't.

Where to sit? Who will fully recline their seat into the next three hours of my life? First I try to identify the people with chicken on their person. Then I look for children who've been hugged too much, and, you know what, adults who've been hugged too much, because my chair's getting kicked either way. I zoom right past anyone with a lanyard around their neck—they will, without fail, clip their fingernails once we're on the turnpike. And, oh my god, I'd rather sit anywhere than next to a girl in a Barnard hoodie with a laptop—I promise you she brought Food from fucking Home, she brought fucking apple slices in a Ziploc bag. A baby Ziploc bag, to match the baby voice in which she will speak to her boyfriend on her cell phone during thesis breaks every fifty miles: "Oh my god, I miss you toooooo. Nothing, I'm just on the *buuuuuuuus*."

One time I sat among a punk rock band. The lead singer leaned over me to flip off the Sallie Mae headquarters as we passed it in Delaware, and as she did one of her dreadlocks curled in my open palm. It felt like a bendy bone, and it upset me.

On a bus home to visit my parents, the man and woman in front of me struck up a conversation. They were both artists who lived in Greenpoint and had seen each other around.

"I'm into death, I'm into death studies," he told her. "Do you know what I did for my twenty-ninth? I dug up my dog. I'd buried him four years ago, but I just wanted his bones so bad. I felt like an archaeologist. I love bones. I have a lot of skulls."

"What about people who've died—do you want their bones?" she asked.

"No," he replied, almost offended by the question. "That would be sad." He started showing her pictures of skulls on his phone. "I'm very eccentric, like Dalí," he noted.

"I was just about to say that," she cooed. "Like Dalí, totally."

"I want to draw you," he said. "May I draw you?"

Thirty minutes later he turned his sketchpad around to show her the result. I leaned forward and peered through the gap between their seats to look as well. She gasped—he'd gone full Edward Gorey and made her look like some sort of hipster gorgon.

"I was trying to play with shadows and light," he explained.

He got her number anyway, and they made dinner plans for when they were both back in Greenpoint.

I try to find the quiet people—practicing monks, fresh induct-ees into the Witness Protection Program, humorless children from Ingmar Bergman films—but I can only assume they're all on the Acela. I swear to god, if I could travel in a cushioned, single-occupancy, sandalwood-scented pod that gently rocked and played the sound of ten progressive mothers *shhh*-ing me, I would be thrilled, and I leave it to the Japanese to design such a method of conveyance.

Cooking for One

- - - - - - -

- *Roasted Vegetable Soup* -

WHAT YOU'LL NEED

3 to 4 cups chicken stock

1 quart roasted winter vegetables (carrots, parsnips, sweet potatoes, butternut squash)

1 roommate on vacation

34 blatant propositions messaged to local gays

0 interested

1 ½ tablespoons of kosher salt, in the wound

Dates

A palm reader I drunkenly went to told me that I'd have four soul mates in my life.

"Really?" I asked, nearly jumping out of my seat with excitement.

She raised a hand of caution. "Well, you know," she added. "Soul mates can also just be friends."

Since they didn't make enough Paul Rudds to go around, the rest of us have to date. I know. It's the worst. It's the absolute worst. Someone once asked me, "Which is worse, writing or dating?" and it's hard to say; they're both such solitary acts.

Here are the stages of a relationship, as I understand them:

The Ask
The Date
The Kiss
The Sex
The End

Between The Sex and The End I've noticed some people choose to add The Trip to Thailand and The Vegan Year, but of course that's their prerogative.

The best place to meet men, I've found, is your mind.

I have a Black-Irish Subway Boyfriend who never looks at me—it's kind of our thing. His arms are always flexed, holding a science fiction novel up to his face. I'll whip out my copy of *Harper's Magazine* and try to make a big show out of also being a "reader," angling it so the cover is visible to him, thereby rendering the magazine's contents completely unreadable to me—but it would all be worth it if he looked up and saw how smart and cultured I am because I'm reading fucking *Harper's*. I stare at him, willing him, *daring* him to look at me, but he doesn't. I try to match his fervor for reading with my own material, which has resulted in my actually learning something about the Sandinistas.

I used to think I was incredibly ballsy, writing my phone number on slips of paper and handing them out left and right to bartenders, waiters, and merchandise managers at Broadway musicals, until my therapist at the time branded my actions decidedly uncourageous. "If your goal was to get them on the phone, you failed," he said, petting his disgusting cat, Clara, which he continually let into the room even after I told him I was allergic. "You should have asked them for *their* phone numbers. I think your goal instead was to feel the most accomplished with the least amount of effort." I never went back, and Clara can choke on a dick.

In college I invited a handsome classmate over to my apartment for dinner and a Pixar movie. I spent the entire movie building up enough courage to, at the end of it, turn to him and say, "I have something to tell you."

"What?" he asked.

I hadn't built up the courage to say the next bit, and it seemed weird to suggest another movie to buy time, so I—oh, god—ran into my bedroom, grabbed a pen and the promotional Lipitor notepad I'd gotten from my aunt who's a nurse, and rejoined him on the couch. On the pad's top sheet I wrote, *I have a crush on you.*

I tore the sheet from the pad and handed it to him: my heart's expression, or a prescription for Lipitor.

He read it. "Oh," he said, and folded it. He looked at me. "I've kind of started seeing Keith," he said—Keith was a handsome classmate of ours—"and things are getting pretty serious. I'm sorry."

He handed the folded note back to me and smiled apologetically. He and Keith have since become engaged, and I've grown even *further* muted in my communications with men. I will now send a Facebook message, which in Jane Austen terms is, like, the equivalent of riding my horse four fields over from the house of my intended and firing my rifle into the sky. At best, my intended would go to the window and be like, "What was that?" and then return to weaving at the loom.

If he asks you whether this is a good Grindr neighborhood, it's not a date. If it's before six o'clock post meridian, it's not a date. If he brings a friend, it's not a date. If he brings the cannibal he's planning on selling you to, it's not a date.

If the cannibal is punctual and has HBO Go, it's a date.

*   *   *

There was once, very briefly, a Gorgeous Spaniard.

He was a performer, and the company he was a member of was doing a show at the theater I work at. One night he was the company's box office liaison, and when I let him inside my office to put his stuff down I admired his coiffure, his glasses, his scruff. He began to speak in seductive, surprising cadences—the words fell out of his mouth like fucking European glitter, and I thrilled to his presence; it had gifted an unremarkable evening with wattage.

We began to banter. I thought to myself, *Don't get carried away, he's way too gorgeous to be into you, flirting is like breathing to a Gorgeous Spaniard, even his farts bat their eyelashes.* And then I thought, *Fuck it, I'm going to get better at this and flirt back a little, for practice, or at least for a memory to cling to irrationally when I'm old and crossing the street with my plastic bag full of other plastic bags.*

And then, as the curtain went up and he was signing the box office reports, he said, "I feel like having a glass of wine before I head home. Would you like to join me for a glass of wine?"

My face got hot, my clothed body parts began to sweat, and my heart fist-bumped my rib cage. It seemed like such a natural question, and it was so smoothly asked, like in a movie or the life of a confident person. I wanted so desperately to say yes.

But I couldn't. I had dinner plans and I didn't want to cancel at such late notice.

"I would love to, but I can't," I said tragically. "What about tomorrow?"

"Okay," he said. "Tomorrow."

As I walked to dinner I felt vibrant and triumphant, like Angela Bassett at the end of all her movies. All throughout dinner I kept thinking about making crazy Almodóvar love to the Gorgeous Spaniard—collapsing in a breathless heap on his kitchen floor in Williamsburg, covered in flour and Spanish wine, tatters of his shirt in my fists and my hoop earring bloody between his teeth.

The following night, when I heard a knock at the box office door, I ran to open it, only to find the company's usual box office liaison standing there.

"Where's Matteo?" I asked.

"He said he had a lot of work to do at home," she said. "What am I, chopped liver?"

Yes, I wanted to say, *you're chopped liver*.

I sank back into my desk chair. He wasn't coming. I realized the movie I was in starred not Angela Bassett but Imelda Staunton. "Could I see your contact sheet again?" I asked as nonchalantly as I could, and she shrugged and forwarded it to me from her phone. I texted him, asking if he'd still like to get a drink sometime, and got no response. A few days later I sent another text. Again: no response.

Did it happen? Was it real? Was he just a dairy-induced hallucination? These are my questions, and I'll never know the answers. Also, how do you get European glitter out of a carpet?

I recently watched the movie *Red Dragon*, in which Ralph Fiennes plays a serial killer who, yes, kills a lot of people, but also develops a fondness for and starts a relationship with a blind woman, played by Emily Watson. She senses scary darkness in him, but cares for him anyway.

I don't fault her. It's a jungle out there, and sometimes the person you meet in the clearing is a serial killer. A serial killer who spares you, which, when you think about it, is pretty romantic. It's not every man who will reckon with the demon he ultimately serves for permission to not bite off your fingers and put mirror shards in your eye sockets. I mean, he's meeting you halfway. He loves putting mirror shards in people's eye sockets.

Do you know how hard it is to meet a man these days who has found his calling? My standards are obviously too high. Yes, he eats the tongues of men, but he's chewing with his mouth closed. Yes, he screams in the night, but at least he's not going on and on about some Internet meme. No, performing oral sex on him as he watches home videos of the next family he's planning on killing is not fun, but neither is blowing a guy after you've seen his cabaret.

My thumb knocked against my wine glass, and as if in slow motion, I watched its contents fly in a wet clump toward my date like a swarm of angry red bees, like a jumping, snapping *West Side Story* wine gang, and land on every single thing he was wearing. It dripped from his glasses a little, rolled down his neck, and plunged below his collar.

"Oh my god," I said, "I am so, so sorry!"

"It's okay," he said, but clearly it wasn't okay, so I said, "No, no, no, it's not okay, your nice shirt, my god!"

I offered to pay for the dry cleaning, told him to Facebook

me the total. He declined, but did at least accept my Tide-to-Go
pen, which he used on the crotch of his pants openly, in front
of me, while I asked for the check. He kept the Tide-to-Go pen,
which was fine; it was part of a two-pack.

If you're tempted to cancel, it's a date.

The guy from OkCupid was half an hour late. It was Decem-
ber, and the restaurant wouldn't seat me—"You're an incomplete
party," the hostess seemed to relish telling me—so I stood outside in the cold.

Upon arrival, he said, "Sorry, I was at an impound lot."

"Oh no, was your car in it?" I asked.

"No," he said, and walked ahead of me to our table. After we
ordered, he put both elbows on the table and said, "So you're
from Baltimore."

"Yes," I replied.

"What's the slogan for Baltimore, something like—?"

"Well, we were The City That Reads for a while, because we
weren't reading, and they wanted to encourage it—"

"No, no, what's it now? Charm City?"

"Yes, Charm City," I said.

He laughed slightly and spun his knife on the table. "I mean,
I wouldn't call it charming. I've seen *The Wire*."

Later, he asked, "Where would you go tomorrow, if money
were no issue?"

"Paris," I said, "I've always wanted to go to Paris."

He rolled his eyes. "*Everybody* wants to go to Paris."

Great, I thought, *we can get a group rate.*

At the end of the meal, as we were splitting the check, he told me, "I was talking with some friends about who should pay for dates. You know, because it's tricky for gay people. There's no, like, Victorian courtship construct."

Fairly certain he'd been waiting the entire meal to use the phrase "Victorian courtship construct," I asked, "And what did you all decide?"

"That the person who asked the other on the date should pay."

"Ah." My hands hovered above the check.

"You know, it's nice to be old-fashioned sometimes."

I nodded. "Well, then, let *me* get this."

"What?" he exclaimed, a hand raised in faux-test. "No. No!"

If you consider not shaving or changing your sheets for it, it's a date.

After two dinners and a sleepover, a cute performance artist put his hand on my knee and asked if we could just be friends.

I felt my face drop. I couldn't stop it. I also felt sweat drop, from anywhere on my body able to produce it, because it was summer and he did not own an air conditioner. He'd said he thought it would make for a great story later in life—you know, *Let me tell you about that crazy summer when I was twenty-two and living in New York without an air conditioner*, and in that moment I thought I was still on a date so I just laughed, and when I laughed a little sweat went into my mouth, but now that I'm not on a date please know that that is the *worst story ever*, and you should get a fucking air conditioner.

It all hurt, but when I got home I cut my hand on a glass and that hurt worse, so: perspective.

If you're panicked that everything's going to change, it's a date.

I led a guy down a maze of West Village streets trying to find the most deserted one. We landed, appropriately, on Gay Street. He chattered amiably about, I don't know, music education in schools or something, and I tried to find a contiguous stretch of townhomes with their lights off in front of which to set up shop. I did, and we stopped, and I'm shy and he was shy, so we just stood in front of people's trash cans for a couple of minutes before I bit the bullet, and his lower lip.

He pulled away and said, "I know why you took me down this street."

"You do?" I said.

"Yeah," he replied. "It's okay, I get it. But we can kiss in front of people, too."

If you feel yourself stepping out like a beat cop in front of even the parts of you that you like and saying "Nothing to see here, move it along," it's a date.

*　　*　　*

"I can't drink tonight," a guy said as we sat down to dinner.

I'd met him at a *Game of Thrones* viewing party for uptown gays. He had a golden smile and promising chest hair and I asked him if he'd like to have dinner with me in the neighborhood some time. He said sure. Where to eat proved an issue: there's really only one good restaurant in the neighborhood, and it's Italian, and he said he doesn't "gravitate toward Italian food," and quite frankly I just don't trust people who don't gravitate toward Italian food, but finally he agreed.

"Why can't you drink?" I asked.

"I'm on antibiotics. An ex of mine called me this morning and said he has a little something, and that *I* might have a little something, too," he said.

I am not exaggerating when I tell you that this was the *first* conversation we had upon sitting. They hadn't even brought over water yet. "What's the little something?" I asked.

He spread his napkin across his lap and patted it smooth. "Gonorrhea."

"Oh, I've had gonorrhea," I offered, thinking it might provide some comfort.

"Me, too," he quipped. "This isn't my first rodeo."

The waitress swung by to take our drink order. My itchy-dicked companion swiped the air with his hand—nothing for him—but told me, "You should drink toni—"

"Could I have a glass of rosé?" I was already asking the waitress.

As our dinner continued he seemed hell-bent on desexualizing the proceedings entirely. "The doctor at the clinic was so weird," he said. "He told me he lived right near me. He gave me his phone number and told me to text him for the results. He told me he was a 'swabbing guy,' and when I unzipped my fly he told me I really filled out a pair of jeans."

"Oh god!" I laughed conspiratorially, wine in hand.

Familiar coils warmed within me as I understood plain and clear, *This isn't a date*, and the sensation I felt was relief. I could calm down; this I could do. I could sip my wine and laugh and ask him questions. I didn't have to worry about kissing him on the street or whether I was supposed to pay for dinner or whether he wanted to spend the night. *You're going to get a pint of ice cream after this*, I told myself, *and then you're going to sit and watch all your stories.*

"So tell me about your ex," I said.

Scene from a Box Office

- - - - - - -

OLDER MAN: Is this a gay play?

ISAAC: (*cautiously*) Yes . . .

OLDER MAN: And . . . not that you would necessarily *know* this, but . . .

ISAAC: Yes?

OLDER MAN: I don't want to offend. I'm in town from Culver City with my friend. Where can we . . . go after the show?

ISAAC: Do you mean a—

OLDER MAN: (*leaning in, whispering*) A gay club. No offense intended, if you aren't.

ISAAC: None taken. I'm very gay. But I'm not good with the clubs, really.

OLDER MAN: Guide us, we are helpless.

ISAAC: Well, there are a ton of places nearby, west of here in Hell's Kitchen.

OLDER MAN: Will we feel uncomfortable? We're in our fifties and we aren't out.

ISAAC: Oh, well, see, I'm out, but I stay in, so you might not want to take my nightlife recommendations.

OLDER MAN: (*leaning in again*) Our hotel is right next to Hunk-O-Mania, and even though I read that they only allow women in, last night I watched a ton of men go in.

ISAAC: It sounds like maybe you should try Hunk-O-Mania, then!

OLDER MAN: (*leaning back*) I'm sorry to trouble you.

ISAAC: Oh, it's no trou—

OLDER MAN: Thank you for your help. (*waving with his ticket envelope, walking quickly away*) Thank you.

Subway Diary

- - - - - - -

A train, 9:30 a.m., Tuesday

"What time do you have to be at work?" a man asks the young woman cuddling him.

"Ten," she says.

"Oh, you should've told me. I would've woken you up earlier."

She giggles. "It's fine."

"I would've gladly paid for a cab."

"Yeah, but I always think, that's, like, twenty-five dollars I could've spent on something else."

"See, I have to force myself to take the subway," he says. "I like the finer things. Guess how much this suit cost?"

She giggles. "I don't know."

"Three thousand," he proclaims. "I was in a cab the other night and I wanted to see if this seafood restaurant on 125th Street was open, so I told him to swing by and he said no. He said he had somewhere to be. I told him, 'Motherfucker, let me out on 125th Street. I pay you to do what I say.'"

"Right, he was disrespecting you," she agrees.

"How old are you?" he asks.

"Thirty-two."

"No way are you thirty-two. You're lying."

"I'm thirty-two!"

"I'm gonna call up *The Maury Povich Show*: 'Fourteen-Year-Old Girl Posing as Thirty-Two-Year-Old Woman.'"

She squeals. "Awww!"

He leans in. "So when can I call you? When is he not home?"

"The mornings," she says.

"Like, from when to when?"

"Like, eight to nine. And then in the evening from six to nine or something."

Smoothing his suit, he says, "Okay. Cool."

6 train, 7:30 p.m., Wednesday

A nicely dressed, one-armed woman reads a magazine quietly. The two-armed woman next to her watches her and, after a moment, leans in. "You people inspire me," she says.

"What?" the one-armed woman asks, looking up.

"You people, just the way you adapt—"

"Oh, no, no, please," the one-armed woman interjects.

"What happened?" the two-armed woman asks.

"Nothing; I was born like this."

"So you've never known any different. Wow."

"'You people' is just a little—" the one-armed woman starts to say, but the two-armed woman looks at the ceiling and murmurs, "Wow, *wow*," then turns back to the one-armed woman and says, "Well, you inspire me. Truly."

The one-armed woman nods a little and looks back at her

magazine. The two-armed woman looks back at the ceiling, placid and smiling, blissed-out.

A train, 10:30 a.m., Friday

I hold the door for an older woman in a newsboy cap and a sharp jacket who doesn't thank me, nor does she quicken her pace. She instead lifts the bottle of cheap vodka she's holding, half-empty (or half-full; I'm really trying to be better about that), and flings its contents at the train as if to bless it.

Once seated, she emits a primal Linda Blair scream—"AHHHHH!"—with her tongue hanging and wagging from her mouth.

At the next stop people file on and find seats, but a larger woman opts to stand. The older woman takes one look at her and recoils. "GET AWAY FROM ME, YOU PIG! YOU THICK BITCH!" she screams, flinging her vodka at the woman, but the cap's on, so it's more of a symbolic gesture. "I'll cut you! I'll cut your head off and PUT AN APPLE IN YOUR MOUTH!" The larger woman finally seeks shelter at the other end of the car.

At the next stop, right under New York-Presbyterian Hospital, two attractive young men in scrubs and messenger bags step on and sit across from her. "Hey," she coos. "Give me a try. I'll take your dick around the world."

A man who's standing turns to get a look at who's saying these things, and she screams at him, "Why are you LOOKING AT ME?" Her voice shatters into varying pitches at the end of each scream. "Stay the fuck AWAY FROM ME!"

She takes another swig of her vodka. "*Don't cry for me, Argentina . . .*" she sings, holding the vodka to her lips like a microphone. "*The truth is I never leave you, all through my bad days, my good days sometimes, I kept my promise . . .* AND YOU BROKE IT!"

She slumps, her heavily made-up face now melting. She looks like an oil painting.

Everybody gives her space.

Triptych

I was in the middle of fellating an aloof actor when suddenly, out of nowhere, he said, "God, I hate Edward Albee."

I popped his dick out of my mouth. "I'm sorry?" I asked.

He propped himself up on his elbows and looked at my books. "You have a bunch of his plays," he said. He'd been completely silent up to this point, which surprised me, since all any actor wants to do is direct.

"Yes, I do." My glasses were off, so I squinted to see what he was referencing. "You really hate him?"

"I don't know. He's just, like, needlessly obtuse." He scratched his stomach. "Sorry, didn't mean to interrupt. You can proceed."

"No, wait," I said, clambering to my feet. "Hand me my glasses. Which plays are you looking at?"

He started coming over regularly. We grew comfortable. One night after we'd finished, I rubbed Eucerin onto my elbows and told him, "You should eat something. Your stomach kept growling."

"I'll heat something up at home," he replied, taking out his contacts and rubbing his eyes. "This is not a fun forty-eight hours for me. I have to get up at five to go be an extra on *The Good Wife*—hand someone a plate in a restaurant or something—and then I have rehearsal until midnight." He whistled. "How's work? You still at the . . . ?"

"Box office," I said, scooting to the edge of the bed next to him. "And yes, I am. It's fine. Are you still hard?"

"Yeah, it takes forever to go down," he muttered. "It's a pain in the ass."

I grabbed his penis and began to tug it, gently. It was heavy like a cheap bodega flashlight in my hand.

"Oh, did I give you a postcard for my show?" he asked.

"You did," I replied. "Last time."

"I think it'll be good. I mean, I think I'll be good. I can't speak for the play or anybody else," he said, thrusting his pain in the ass farther into my grip, "but I'm gonna be good."

"Before we get started," a handsome hedge-funder said, taking a seat at the edge of my bed, "I just want to clear the air about something."

He removed his baseball cap. There was a large gash on his forehead. It looked like a strip of bacon. I couldn't help it—I gasped, and he flinched.

"See, you noticed it immediately, I knew you would," he muttered.

"What on earth happened?" I asked.

"A horse kicked me in the head," he said.

"Oh my god. Really?"

"Yes."

"Don't people, like, die from that?" I was trying to look any-where but at the gash.

"Not me." He began to unbutton his shirt.

"Do you work with horses?"

"Fuck no," he said. "I was playing polo."

Right. Hedge fund. "And you're all right?"

"I'm fine," he said, clearly tired of discussing it. "I just can't listen to my iPod too loud."

"Well, I'll try to keep the loud noises and sudden movements to a minimum," I said.

"Very funny," he said, not laughing.

"Don't want to trigger any dormant rage!"

"Let's move on."

"Okay."

After unleashing what felt like a Nickelodeonic amount of cum onto my face, the lanky, half-white, half-Asian guy from Grindr asked, "Got a towel?"

My eyes closed tight, I gestured to the box of tissues on my bookshelf and heard him pull one out. I was about to stand and fumble blindly for my own tissue when I felt his hand cup my chin. He tilted my face up and gently wiped himself from my eyes. He stepped away, and I heard him pull a second and third tissue from the box, and then he was back again, wiping my forehead, my cheeks, my weak jawline and chin. He stopped near my mouth, making sure that it was indeed a scar beneath my nose—the kindergarten playground asphalt's doing, not his.

Neither of us said a word. When I opened my eyes he was

balling up the tissues and tossing them into my trash can as if he was a surgeon just out of the operating room. "You're gonna make it," I half expected him to say. And, for once, I felt like I might.

"What's your name?" I asked him.

His pace was different now. He quickly grabbed for his clothes and began to put them on. "Matthew," he replied. "What's yours?"

"Isaac," I said, starting to dress as well. "What do you do, Matthew?"

"I'm a *writ-ah*," he said in a British accent.

I laughed. "Oh? I'm a *writ-ah*, too."

He shook his head as he put on his left sock and, still in a British accent, asked, "Are you making fun of my accent?"

I realized it was the first I'd really heard him speak since he arrived. "Oh god, sorry, are you actually British?" I asked.

"Yep," he replied, pulling on his running shorts.

"What do you write?"

"Short stories." His shirt was on. "You?"

"Plays, essays, poems, stuff. Have you read any Alice Munro?"

"Who?" He was looking for his keys.

"She's basically *the* short-story writer."

"Ah, I think I might've read her at uni; don't remember, though." His keys found, he now stood at the door.

"Well," I said, turning to my bookshelf and scanning the spines, "I have all of Alice Munro's collections here if you want to read . . ."

He put his hands to his head. "Sorry, I'm a blur tonight. I'm really stoned, and I wasn't really expecting to have to talk about writing."

I walked him to the door. He stepped out into the hall and looked each way.

"Make a left?"

"Right," I corrected.

He went left.

"No, *make* a right," I called to him.

He made a right, and as he passed me again, said, "Cheers."

"Cheers," I said.

Some Scattered Thoughts on Los Angeles, Las Vegas, and Marion, Massachusetts

----

I was recently in Los Angeles for a horrid process called "taking meetings," as if meetings were good for you, like vitamins. I sat in a sleek and shiny office underneath towering posters of Jim Carrey and Will Ferrell, sipping the sparkling water I'd been handed by a toothsome assistant in a headset and morning scruff. "Britta's ready to see you," he said.

I sat with Britta and did my best not to burp up sparkling water. Britta was beautiful—she looked rested, fed, unafraid. People don't really look like that in New York, not even the hugely successful ones. "Your work," she said, tapping her pen on her desk. "It's a little gay-heavy, but it's still funny."

I reached for my murse, figuring the meeting was unequivocally over, but she continued to make small talk, perhaps to fluff the meeting out to a less-insulting fifteen minutes. "Oh, we just started repping Andrew Rannells," she said. "Do you know him? He's also—"

"Gay?" I asked.

"No—well, yes, but no," she said, laughing. "I was going to say from New York."

The meetings aside, I really loved Los Angeles. Every day was sixty-five degrees and sunny with no humidity and a constant galvanizing breeze. This weather, I'm told, lasts almost year-round, except for two pesky months when it's 120 degrees and everything catches on fire. I'd hoped for some Carole King Quality Time along the Pacific Coast Highway, maybe thirty-five minutes or so of gentle weeping, but it made my friend Dave, who I was traveling with, uncomfortable.

Everywhere we went there were people to park the car, and you have to "get validated," something I thought could only be done through anonymous sex. There were medical marijuana prescriptions for anxiety, something all of my friends who've moved out there suddenly suffer cripplingly from. There were young men in Ray-Bans with Vasco da Gama mustaches—what are they discovering, exactly, besides new music? I misread an address and walked for forty-five minutes along Sunset Boulevard, which is apparently not something people ever do in Los Angeles. I encountered maybe two other pedestrians in total, and it would not be long before they were back in the state's care.

Other hotels in Las Vegas had headliners like Elton John and Rod Stewart. Mine had Criss Angel and Carrot Top, enough to turn your sex organs into Sylvia Plath. I was there for my boss's wedding and stayed in the Luxor, an Egyptian-themed hotel at the south end of the Strip that's shaped like a pyramid. The world's brightest light beam shoots up from the pyramid's point, presumably so all the people stumbling around the lobby in margarita helmets can find it.

I love Las Vegas. It has all my favorite things: big hotels, the indoors, restaurants, games, places to sit. Context is roundly discouraged. If you miss daylight, there are plenty of hotels that will simulate it for you on their ceilings. And if you'd rather not walk, giant conveyer belts can carry you and your margarita helmet out of a hotel, up over the highway, and right into another hotel that's playing the same Not Quite Katy Perry music as the last.

I saw formal trackwear. I saw a man using his drink as a cane. I saw about forty-eight men I'd like to hate-blow in the Paris casino alone. A showgirl posing in her skimpies on the sidewalk asked a mother and father how old their son was. "Oh, mine's three," she then said. "He's always going for my camera, too."

At every street corner a cavalcade of flyer guys for area strip clubs muttered rhythmically as we passed, "Steak and titty, steak and titty."

"No, thank you," I said.

"We've got guys dancing, too," one of them replied.

There was a Marine ball at the Mirage, and a Marine asked me if I wanted to buy him a drink. At first I was tempted, since many gay porns commence in such a manner, as do hate crimes, so I pretended not to hear him.

I ate orange chicken among Egyptian ruins and snow crab legs in a French town square. At a breakfast buffet I filled my plate with pumpkin pancakes next to Not Quite Kardashians whose leopard-print dresses from the night before could no longer contain *their* pumpkin pancakes.

As fun as Vegas is, three days there was more than enough. The simulated times of day and conditioned climates may have fooled most of me, but my eczema, ever intuitive and opportunistic, exploded around my ankles and elbows. It knew the simple arid truth: that underneath it all, Vegas is a flash of pleasure, a furious quenching of thirst in the middle of a desert.

I was in Marion, Massachusetts, for a long weekend with my friend Marianna at her family's house. I'd hoped, being so close to Cape Cod, that I could at least have a maid to fire or a husband to resent as I vigorously hand-washed some organic grapes, but no such luck.

I'd forgotten how fucking hard swimming is. We swam in the harbor, and luckily there was a lifeguard on a nearby dock. Even though my glasses were ashore I could still make out a blur of hair on his chest, and I was kept afloat by my buoyant lust.

We went sailing, a first for me. My nautical duties included switching sides whenever one side of the boat needed more weight (ouch), waving to every boat that passed (apparently mariners' feelings are easily hurt), and taking gallons of saltwater to the face every thirty seconds (I swear we were in a white squall). I screamed my head off until I realized someone might call the harbormaster and report a kidnapped girl.

We rode bikes into town. I was on a tandem bike with Marianna's cousin's husband, Pablo, and the backseat came with far more control than I was expecting—I'd been hoping for more of a sidecar situation—and I was causing the bike to swerve wildly.

"Relax your hips," Pablo kept saying to me, but he'd met me only a day earlier and didn't yet know how lost *that* cause is.

Subway Diary

A train, 11:00 a.m., Thursday

Forty women in matching lime-green T-shirts fill the train, hooting and hollering. They hold bullhorns and signs that say "LATCH ON NYC!" and one of them carries a life-sized cardboard cutout of a woman in an evening gown breastfeeding an infant.

"It's Breastfeeding Awareness Week!" the woman closest to me shouts.

I turn off my Judy Collins and listen.

"Chant with me!" she continues, and they all chant, *"Mommies know it's nutritious! Babies know it's delicious!"*

A photographer with weathered credentials hanging from his neck moves among them, snapping away, while a reporter from NPR interviews the woman holding the cardboard cutout. The woman leading the chants, obviously smarting from NPR's interview choice, takes it up a notch and just starts shouting, "WHOO! WHOO!" into her bullhorn.

One of the women actually has a baby, and she sits and begins to breastfeed it. The reporter and photographer flock to her, and the chant leader, no fool, goes as well, seizing her moment. "What she's doing is healthy and perfectly natural!" she shouts into the bullhorn. "If you see a woman in public feeding her child, give her a pat on the back and say 'Thank you for nourishing your child!'"

I make eye contact with a few people, and we're all like, *We will* not *be doing that, but thanks.*

Suddenly, a man farther down the car shouts, "I SUPPORT YOU!"

"*Yeah!*" the women cheer.

"I SUPPORT YOU!" he repeats, standing.

The women surround him. "*Yeah!*"

"GIVE ME A TASTE!" he shouts.

"*Ye—*" the women start, then recoil en masse and descend upon him, unleashing a collective reprimanding scream. He covers his head, shielding himself.

F train, 1:30 p.m., Friday

"I'm thinking about flying to California for the weekend," a leather-voiced woman says to her friend.

"You got money for that?" her friend asks.

"I will. Fred's been bad."

"Oh, shit. How bad?"

"Napa bad. I've got him trained. He does something bad, he gets out the checkbook and writes five and three zeros. I make him do it in front of me. I like to watch him sign the checks. He whines like a little bitch every time and tries to haggle, as if the rate is negotiable."

"I'm jealous," her friend says. "You've got it good."

"Seriously!" the woman hoots. "I'm like, 'Cheat on me again! Give me chlamydia; I want a Dior bag!'"

C train, 11:00 p.m., Thursday

"I gotta ask," a middle-aged man says to me. "Are you gay?"

I nod.

"I thought so, from the way you were sitting."

I nod again. "Okay."

"What do you do?"

"I'm a writer."

"Oh, I want to be a writer, too."

"Nice," I say.

He scratches at his head. "I have a story I want to write called 'Wrigley's.'"

I just keep nodding. "Okay, cool."

"Yeah, it's about how this friend of my dad's would lure us down to the basement as kids and touch us. He'd always give us a stick of Wrigley's at the end and tell us not to tell nobody."

"Oh my god," I say.

"Yeah," he continues, "I know you're gay and all, and I just always think, maybe I'd be gay on my own, maybe I'd have the opportunity to figure out what I liked and didn't like on my own, but I didn't get that." He looks up. "This is my stop. Good luck with your writing."

The Horny New York Poem

———————

Amorous vegans mill freshly outside of Angelica Kitchen
like the oats they're waiting for.
A husband rides his bicycle along Houston,
his wife in the basket.
Jäger-bombed brawn rules the Bowery.
A woman poses in the window of the Crosby Street Hotel,
a hand squarely on each hip—
a dominatrix,
or at least trying to think like one.

The night breeze is a warm exhale,
an olive branch.

We've peeled ourselves from our desks
where we sat all day like spilled soda,
and stumbled, sweaty zombies, out into the night.

Overheard on Ninth Avenue:
"How'd you meet?"
"Twitter."

On Sixteenth Street:
"Why is he calling you?"
"Oh, I gave to his Kickstarter."

On Bank Street:
"You'll never leave her."
"I will."

A man in a passing car shouts,
"Yo, that fag is gay!" or "Yo, that bag is gay!"
It's unclear.
I bet he kicked himself for that confusion.
"What a mouth full of marbles I have!"
he probably said.

On Curry Row young brothers Lehman
massage each other's bespoke-suited shoulders
as maître d's bark and beckon them inside.

On Second Avenue women wilt like petals
from bar stool stems.

In front of Sunshine Cinema
a woman screams at a man,
"You cannot just *desert* your family in New York City!"
and he whispers, "You're gonna go to jail again,"
and she says, "It'll be WORTH IT."

The arriving train whips the scent of the man in front of me

on the platform

up my nostrils

to my calloused receptors,

and I think, *Okay, tonight.*

A man across from me cuddles a woman

and tells her, "You're skinny because I love you all night."

An actress, still in her show makeup,

a face for the back of the house,

brings a kale smoothie to her boyfriend's lips.

A teenaged couple neck and text

on the stained couch in the Laundromat.

In my room, the man I just met

sits naked on my bed

looking at my books,

Toni Morrison inches from his inches.

I've just returned with waters,

which I set down for later,

and in I go,

in we all go,

to give it another go,

to lie down and be counted.

The White Russian

The semi-intense language barrier between the Russian ballroom dance instructor and me got things off to a rocky start, what with him looking at me and smiling blankly and me saying everything two different ways—"I'm a playwright; I write plays," and "I've been living here for five years; five years in Washington Heights," and "This is my bedroom; this is where I sleep"—and I continued to yammer on until he just, I don't know, touched my face and said, "Do not speak because of nervous," and leaned in and kissed me.

I nearly cried.

Afterward we watched YouTube videos of him ballroom dancing. I showed him the video of that girl Scarlett taking a tumble off of her coffee table, which thankfully holds up in all languages. We downed shots of cold vodka in my living room and played tennis on my Wii—to this day his Mii character is still part of my Wii posse.

"Do you want to spend the night?" I asked him at around three thirty.

He shook his head, smiling. "I teach early," he replied. "I teach the children."

"Okay," I said, zipping up his jacket for him. "Go teach the children."

"The children try my patience."

"Children do that."

"I do not want to have children."

I put a hand on my hip. "Okay, we don't have to have children."

He looked at me quizzically. "Good night, nervous," he said.

A few nights later he was again in my bed. "What is this 'night owl'?" he asked me.

"It's when you like to stay up late," I explained.

"Having sex?"

"Well, sure, that could be one thing you do."

"Why are you owl?"

"Because owls like the night, and so do I . . . ?"

"What are you in daytime?"

"Well, I'm the same; I just like staying up late."

He nodded. "You are a funny night owl." He started to hump my leg. "Unh," he moaned with each thrust. "Unh, unh."

"What are you, a dog?" I asked.

"No, I am owl. Like you."

"You're humping my leg."

"I am *such an owl.*"

"I don't know about that!"

He stopped and stared at me.

"What?" I asked. He smiled. "What are you doing?" I asked again.

Shaking his head, he replied, "Thinking."

I curled up to him. "What are you thinking about?"

He sighed and looked at the ceiling. "Russia."

"Oh," I said.

Scene from a Box Office

- - - - - - -

BOTOXED MOTHER: What's the holiday show you have coming up?

ISAAC: It's an African circus show . . .

BOTOXED MOTHER: (*to her toddler daughter*) Aurora, *no*, get away from that fountain. Mommy has your filtered water, and Mommy has your croissant and your pesto pasta. Come here, angel.

ISAAC: It's a circus show called *Mother Africa* . . .

BOTOXED MOTHER: Oh, that would be *wonderful*; Aurora is half-African. (*to her daughter*) Aurora, get away from that door. I don't like you near that door. (*to Isaac*) I get her on Saturdays. Do you have Saturday shows?

ISAAC: We do, yes.

BOTOXED MOTHER: (*to her daughter*) Do you want to see a circus show about where Daddy's from? No! Take your, take your hand *out* of that trash can. I can't believe what a little monster you're being! (*to Isaac*) Can you break a hundred?

ISAAC: I can, yes.

BOTOXED MOTHER: See, Mommy's buying you more things. Mommy's been buying you so many things. You've been running Mommy all over town for you. It's like she's your slave. This show should be called *Mommy Africa*. (*to Isaac*) Could I get a receipt? I have to show proof of where I take her on my days.

Home Invasions

When we hatched our plan to have video sex on Skype, I didn't quite grasp that the man and I would *see* and *hear* each other. Not only did I have to throw off my Snuggie, I had to change into better underwear, as though he were actually coming over. He had a great body, that's for sure, but he refused to show his face, which made me wonder if he was famous, and then I decided he was indeed famous, that he was James McAvoy, because why not, I took off my Snuggie for this.

To similarly obscure my face, I angled my webcam down, only to realize ten minutes later that he could now see the block of cheese on the plate next to my keyboard that I'd been enjoying while watching the Kennedy Center Honors.

My radiator kept clanging, so we had to ask each other to repeat what was just said. I could hear other people instant-messaging him on Manhunt. I got a text and checked it. He wanted to look at my ass, which meant I had to turn away from the keyboard and face the framed photograph of John Updike I have on my wall. It's unnerving to slap your ass while looking at John Updike and hearing a disembodied voice from your computer moan in approval. I have a desk chair that spins, so I thought it would be novel to squat on the chair and gyrate a little, giving him a rotating view. That got him to at least stop typing to other people, so I felt victorious until my chair spun too far and I hit my head on my closet door.

The concerned disembodied voice: "Are you okay?"

Me, embarrassed, trying to recover the mood: "Fuck yeah."

At that point I just wanted to get back into my Snuggie and finish my cheese. He told me, "Bend over your bed and get ready for me," which I'm pretty sure was just a way for him to get me out of earshot so he could respond to all the instant-messages that had been piling up during my chair show. I could faintly hear him typing away while I was bent over my bed, moaning and folding my laundry.

Home invasions are one of my biggest fears. I don't mean simple burglaries. I'm talking psychotic-symbolic breaches, like in the movies—you know, where some sicko sets out to punish modern bougie excess one house at a time—which is why I try to make my home life as much of a drag as possible, in case there's a potential invader at the window: *No trips to Aspen being planned in here! Just eating a bowl of Crispix in the dark!* Often is the night that I lie in bed, worrying that the footsteps in the hallway are not the loafers of my pianist neighbor but the soleless boots of soulless men who will kick in the door and torture me, or, even worse, not touch me at all and say they'd rather just be friends.

So I am not the person with whom you should be enacting a home-invasion sex fantasy. The fetish eludes me.

And yet there I was, at the apartment of a man I did not know, opening the front door that he'd left unlocked for me. Once inside, I followed the only apparent light to its source, his bedroom, where he wanted me to "happen upon" him. I slowly pushed open the door and, sure enough, there he was, prostrate and naked on his bed. I figured at this point we could drop the charade and proceed like normal adults with emotional issues, but when he rolled over I noticed he'd blindfolded himself with an Hermès necktie.

I paused. This was not part of the plan. I'd never hooked up with a blindfolded person before, someone with no care for what I might look like in real life.

Do I say hello? I wondered. *Do I make my presence known?* It was clear the level of anonymity he sought was total, so I kept quiet and awkwardly began to undress. My belt hitting the floor was Civil War loud. Saliva caught in my throat, and I tried to pass off the subsequent cough as a titillating grunt. Gay Oedipus stirred on the bed.

Finally naked, I stared down at him. I thought he might say something or do something, but he didn't, so I sat on his face to ease the tension. (Gentle readers, of the many things I wish for you, the first is that at some point in your lives you, too, get to rest your taints on Hermès.) For a minute or two it was as if I'd sat on an unmanned garden hose, but when I grabbed his dick he steadied himself. I generally think sixty-nining is pointless chaos, but it was our only means of communication—a writhing nine tongue-stabbing in the dark, and a six shouldering the sight burden.

He came, and I learned that you can fake a male orgasm when your partner's got Hermès around the eyes. We collapsed next to each other, and he removed his blindfold and smiled goofily at me. "*Hi*," he said, with deep significance, as if he'd run to meet me at an airport at the end of a movie, and kissed me.

He pulled away and kept smiling, so I said hi back, and couldn't really think of anything else to say, because what can you say to someone whose tie you just ruined, but he didn't seem to mind; he sighed, as if to say *What more is there to say? We've said it all already*, and smiled some more, and frankly it was all starting to get a little Landmark-y, so I kissed him again to buy time and plan my escape.

That's when I heard a key in his front door.

"Who's that?" I asked, pulling away.

"My roommate," he said.

"Don't you want to close the door?" I suggested, a bit panicked. "He'll see us."

He shrugged and smiled even wider. "No biggie. He's a modern dancer."

Okay, the *last* person I want seeing me naked is a modern dancer. Fuck that shit. Unless it's an *actually* blind modern dancer—a blind modern dancer who's never been on a roller coaster before and teaches me to see the world in a new way and has such calloused fingers that when he touches my face he thinks I look like Andrew Garfield.

His roommate was having trouble unlocking the door. "Oh, you must have locked the top lock when you came in," he said, hopping off the bed.

"Was I not supposed to?" I called after him.

"No, we never lock it," he replied, and trotted off down the hallway, the darkness engulfing his bare ass.

I called after him, "Are you going to answer the door naked?!"

He called back, "Yeah, we're naked all the time!"

Fucking god, I thought, *it's hippie madness in here. They are just* asking *to get home invaded.*

I looked at my dick and panicked. You do *not* leave a WASP naked in plain sight—we'll shatter into a thousand tiny off-white pieces. I crossed my legs, but I looked like I was waiting for a Caesar salad, so I hugged my knees to my chest, trying to look like Keira Knightley on the Tom Ford *Vanity Fair* cover. No dice. I hid behind his door.

His roommate shuffled off to his own room, probably naked as well, why not. Gay Oedipus came back and snuggled among his pillows. I dressed quickly and desperately. I would have put on all the world's clothes if I could.

"Oh, are you leaving?" he asked over his shoulder, once it was undeniably clear that yes, I was leaving. He insisted on walking me to the door, his dick swinging to and fro in front of us like a well-oiled lantern down his dark hallway.

"You should lock your top lock," I said to him at the door, and he gave me another goofy grin before closing it. As I waited for the elevator, I heard him turn only one lock, the bottom one. I shook my head. Can't say I didn't warn him.

A month or so later, an attractive young citizen of New Jersey coaxed me back onto Skype. He wrote to me on Manhunt, and he'd used commas, so, naturally, I was his for the night. He looked like what I imagine the Brawny Paper Towel Man would look like if he were undecided at a state school.

We started off well. Even while talking dirty I could tell he was using commas. He asked me to suck my fingers, which—funny he should ask—I'd just been doing, to get off the seasoning from some Red Hot Blues tortilla chips. I said, "I can do you one better than that," and ran to the Basket o' Stuff behind my bed, rooted through my creams and salves and balms, and pulled out my pink dildo. I ran back to the computer with it. He was thrilled.

"Awesome," he said. "Suck it. Pretend it's me."

"Oh, I'm going to," I responded. I held it up so he could see it, then put my mouth on it and began to go to town.

I hadn't noticed before—but soon did—that it had been so long since I'd had sufficient ceremony to use my pink dildo that it was covered in dust. *Dust.* My mouth and throat were filling with *dust.* I spat out the dildo and gagged, in full view on Skype.

"Damn, someone's eager," he said, and I choked out, "No, it's—one sec," and ran coughing to the bathroom, where I rinsed out my mouth.

"Where'd you go?" I could hear him calling from my computer. I sensed that I was losing my audience, a cardinal sin in my business of show, so I hurriedly washed the dildo with my aloe and green tea hand soap and ran back into my room, on-camera again.

"You okay?" he asked.

I didn't even respond. I just popped that dildo back into my mouth—and gagged *again*, because my *god*, ALOE AND GREEN TEA HAND SOAP BURNS YOUR MOUTH LIKE ACID. I ran back into the bathroom, threw the dildo to the floor, and flushed my mouth out with water and mouthwash and anything holy.

"Hello?"

I could hear him again from the computer.

"You there? Hello?"

I crawled on my hands and knees back into my bedroom so he wouldn't see me and reached up from the floor to quit out of Skype.

I mean, there was no saving that.

Cooking for One

- *Penne al Dente with Olive Oil & Garlic* -

WHAT YOU'LL NEED

¾ pound penne pasta

2 ½ tablespoons good olive oil (although who knows what's good
anymore; it's all so corrupted, an article somewhere said once)

1 ½ tablespoons minced garlic

4 episodes Twin Peaks, *watched through fingers*

2 hours sleep

0 remaining innocence

Love in the Time of Eczema

- - - - - - -

For those of you unfamiliar with it—perhaps because Life is still weighing the most effective way to break you—eczema is a skin disorder. It's common, but should be suffered self-righteously. Scaly red rashes bubble up from the skin and proceed to itch and ache, blister and ooze, crack and bleed. Chief among eczema's many causes are dry wintry air, woolen fabrics (which gives shopping in J. Crew a vegetarian-in-the-butcher-shop mystique), and fragranced soaps, lotions, and detergents (you know, the things that draw people closer to you).

There are additional triggers it's recommended you curb—booze, caffeine, and stress, for example—but give me a fucking break. My doctor told me I needed to start living more "holistically," and I was like MY, MY, LOOK AT THE TIME. Honestly, life is too short, and I'm *fine* waking up with a little blood on the sheets if that is the cost of wine, coffee, and my beloved constant, fear.

However, there's one final, more complicated cost. In sexual scenarios, eczema is considered by most to be a mood inhibitor, a buzz-kill, a why-does-my-touch-make-you-bleed moment.

Never fear. Here, culled from my arguably extensive field experience, is how to have sex with eczema:

Don't. Develop interests, pursuits. You ever been to the Frick?

If you *must* have sex, fine. See if you can find a lover from the unscented-lotion-fetish community. Please note that this is a microcommunity into which some of us have been making inroads for years, so single men don't last long. Try also: swaggering dermatologists, men with no fingertips or eyes. If your dry, bloody hands are coming up empty, attract a man the usual way—by lying.

Layer up. Sleeves to the fingernails, pants tucked into socks, hood and cape. Stevie Nicks meets Edvard Munch.

Go to dinner. Order oolong tea and yogurt, officially the only fucking things that don't trigger an outbreak. Lead with your personality and downplay your body. "Blah blah *bodies*. I'm told companionship in old age is a better investment!" is something you might say as he tries his duck entrée and you force down another cold swallow of yogurt.

Insist upon consummation at your place. If you are not able to properly cloak and obscure the many ointments and liniments surrounding your bed, tell him you are subletting this room from the English Patient.

Draw the curtains as quickly as possible. Outside light is not permitted. Moon? What the fuck is a moon? I'll tell you what the moon is: it's a tattletale. Hermetically seal the curtains to the wall. Slice your lamp cords as he's taking off his shoes in the hallway. He should enter your room the way Clarice Starling entered Buffalo Bill's basement. If he's frightened, good; you want to squirrel away power now.

With him on your bed, kneel in the far corner. Throw your

voice. Shout sweet nothings at him as he undresses. If he asks why you are all the way across the room, tell him you're a pointillist and you're so turned on right now.

Under no condition are his hands to touch your body. Restrain him at each wrist and plant his hands firmly above his head. Hover above him like an apparition. Do not, I repeat, do *not* let your bodies touch unnecessarily, and by that I mean anything outside of penetration—and, quite frankly, see if he can do that without being inside you.

If his hands somehow come loose from your grip and do touch your body, pray it's in a nondisordered area, like the bottom of your foot or the inside of your eye socket. If he does indeed graze your eczema and he is blind, try to pass it off as a poem you wrote about him in Braille and cross your fingers that the words your raised rash spells are inspired and not pedestrian. If he grazes your eczema and he is not blind, and you don't have a relief map of Chile at hand, no need to turn on a light—you can hear a face fall in the dark.

Start over with someone else. You never know. Someday your hand might accidentally caress a dry, rough patch on the left shoulder of the man you're in bed with, and just as he starts to say, "No, it's not what you think—I fell into some quinoa earlier," you'll place a scabbed finger to his lips, rewire and turn on a light, show him your pale upper arm that is striped red like a candy cane, and lock that shit down.

Subway Diary

----

3 train, 3:30 p.m., Friday

"Why are we fighting a war?" the crazy man across from me shouts. "Cancer's the fucking terrorist! Somebody bomb cancer!"

He begins to pace up and down the car. "Who here on this motherfuckin' train can tell me when they're gonna die? No one. You there, hi: you gonna die. And so are you. Loosen up."

He sits back down and eyes a group of college girls. "You think you're so hot, you girls in your skirts," he says. "I've got news for you: when that skirt comes off on the toilet, that's not flowers, that's fuckin' *shit* comin' out of your ass."

L train, 6:00 p.m., Saturday

Three guys are walking up and down the car, selling their CD.

"Do you like rap music? We don't demean women!" they say. "Five dollars! Only five dollars!"

A woman demurs and says, "I already have one of your CDs in my purse, but thank you."

"That wasn't us, ma'am," one of them replies. "Those were different black guys."

E train, 1:30 p.m., Wednesday

"She's going crazy now," the man across from me complains.

"How so?" his friend asks.

"She thinks I'm cheating on her. She's convinced. The funny thing is, I didn't talk about her for, like, the first six months we were together. I didn't tell anyone. I kept it quiet. Now I shout her from the rooftops," he says. "You'd think she'd be pleased. But no, she thinks I'm cheating."

"She doesn't believe you?"

"No, she wants to know why I'm posting about her on Facebook so much now," he continues. "Like that's a bad thing. I'm like, 'Because I want everyone to know I love you,' and she's like, 'No, it's because you're trying to throw me off your trail.'"

"That's cold."

"Seriously."

"Well, are you cheating?"

"What?" he asks.

Ah Ah

I texted and sexted with an adorable young Portuguese mathematician I met online who was fresh out of MIT and interviewing for consulting jobs at hedge funds in the city. Now, I full-on failed a remedial math course in college, so I'm no Einstein, but I knew that hedge fund + MIT + Portuguese = rich, smart girth. And I never took physics, but I knew that if I threw myself at him with enough desperation, there was a chance I might adhere.

So I did. And I did.

The texts were hot, and his English was far better than I'd hoped, although instead of "ha ha" he would type "ah ah," like a horny Count from *Sesame Street*. He was staying with extended family in New Jersey until he got a job, which made sneaking out tricky and gave our correspondence a flashlight-under-the-sheets joie de vivre.

Back and forth we texted, describing the things we would do to each other once we were together in the flesh, *ah ah*, and after a while our texts turned to Portugal, his family, his time at school. I told him what creative nonfiction was, and he told me what long division was. When he texted that he was at the Met with his aunt and uncle, I told him to go to the martini bar on the roof, and he said he'd wait and take me instead. To the untrained eye, as mine apparently remains after all these years, *ah ah*, it would seem that we were connecting beyond the carnal.

So when he suggested Friday night for our first meeting, I Google-calendared that shit so fast. When he suggested in a subsequent text that we go to the Met on Saturday morning ("a backward date, fucking and then museum, ah ah," he wrote), I put that in my Google calendar as well. Both events on the calendar were pink, because that is the coded color of my Life category, and this is my life. *I have a date*, I thought, *a backward date, but a date nonetheless!*

On Friday I woke up early and laundered a towel and pillowcase for him. At work I studied the unibrow and treasure trail in his pictures on my phone. The lady at the wine store helped me find a bottle of pinot gris, his favorite, and she seemed thrown that I was looking for more than just my usual something cheap to wash the cheese down. I did the dishes and cleaned the air conditioner filter and dabbed a little peppermint oil on the four corners of my bed, remembering only afterward that I own the peppermint oil not because it's an aphrodisiac but because it's a homeopathic mouse deterrent.

He was handsome in person, and a little shy, or so I thought. We shook hands. I got out two glasses and poured the wine, and when I looked up his unibrow was furrowed. "What?" I asked.

"I am surprised you actually got wine," he responded.

"We talked about having it," I said. He swished it around in his mouth and made a face. "What?" I asked again.

"It is just okay," he said.

"I don't know a whole lot about wine," I said, and he shrugged, holding the glass up to his nose. He flinched a little, and in that moment I wondered if he only *appeared* to have a unibrow because his eyebrows were always scrunched together, making a goddamn face.

I steered the conversation away from the wine, which I continued to drink even though he didn't, trying to make contact with the person who'd suggested this backward date in the first place. I asked him about the hedge fund life, about going to school in Boston, about the United States in comparison to Portugal. He scoffed when I brought up Jonathan Franzen, which was fine, because I'm sure Jonathan Franzen would scoff at him. He did, at the very least, recite for me his favorite poem, self-translated from the Portuguese, and he prefaced his recitation with a romantic "I highly doubt you've heard of this poem."

And then he started rubbing his crotch, and I remembered: *Oh, right, people will say and promise anything to get off*. All that wine and Met talk was foreplay, and there we were, two people in different stories on the same couch. I decided to get drunk, and was able to ignore him for a while until he started meeting my eyes and then dropping his head to look at the bulge in his jeans. The bulge *was* remarkable, and the pinot gris was effective in addition to being just okay, so I took him into my bedroom, figuring he might still be of use to me.

His kisses were dispassionate (apparently he had learned nothing growing up so close to Spain) and his nipples were also wine snobs. His dick, while impressive and thick, quite frankly smelled. I pulled down his foreskin and, sure enough, there was a small bit of dried semen there. How I relished being able to hold something of his to *my* nose and make a face. I wiped it off, then jerked him and tongued his balls until he came, which thankfully did not take long, seeing as how he was twenty-one and his age group's largest exports are cum and smart remarks.

He mumbled something about the A train and not wanting to be inconsiderate to his aunt and uncle, gathered his things, and left. For a math whiz, you'd think he would've subtracted himself from my apartment a little more smoothly, *ah ah*.

I had forgotten how when you're twenty-one you think you know everything. *Get older*, I wanted to tell him. *You start to know less*.

Love Poem for the Fair-Haired Young Man Doing the *New York Times* Crossword Puzzle

– – – – – – –

What's a two-letter word for
someone who loves you?
"Me."

I do crosswords, too—
albeit the free ones on my
discontinued phone
where "abortion alternative"
is a clue in every other puzzle,
but crosswords nonetheless.

My god, you're doing the *Times* Thursday
in pen?
While you've got that pen poised,
here's our marriage license;
I want that mind in my house.

I can see it now:
you and me and the dogs
all wrapped up in afghans like mummies
at our house up in Maine—
tree branches leaning on the moaning eaves,
winter stew simmering on the stove top,
raccoons burning to death in the chimney.

You'd put your pen down, look up at me,
and say,
"Hey, honey, what's a three-letter
suffix in taxonomy?"
and I'd say,
"How the fuck should I know?
I went to school for theater,
but let me know if you need an
eight-letter abortion alternative,"
and then we'd hold hands
and watch British television
while outside
our taps collected maple sap
and the wolves circled and howled
at the aurora borealis.
Look, I've never been to Maine,
I'm only guessing at what goes on there—
not to mention
I've got three tubs of recently purchased hummus
in this bag
and I'm not expecting guests.

What I'm getting at is,
most people would feel confident
answering in pen
that you would improve my life.

Where I Live

- - - - - - -

There are 133 steps between the platform of my neighborhood subway station and the street. Every evening I climb them, and every evening they wind me. All the other commuters emerge from the station with their dignity intact, having ridden the escalators, while I come up gasping and flailing as if I just fought off an assailant. It's the only exercise I get, though, so I force myself to do it. Slowly and steadily I climb up the middle of the staircase, avoiding the tacit rat lanes at each edge. More often than not, one or two of them will also be making the slow climb, and I imagine them carrying little rat briefcases and rat purses, eager to get home and shake off their little day.

I live on the fourth floor of a prewar building in a neighborhood called Washington Heights. It's where George Washington defended New York against the British in the American Revolution, at Fort Washington, the highest point in Manhattan, which is now a playground where entitled toddlers skirmish with their damaged, simpering parents.

Mine is a modest two-bedroom apartment where air goes to die in the summer and the radiators explode in the winter. There are high ceilings and really fabulous original molding on all the walls and lots of closet space. The apartment's previous tenants were a mother and her hacker son, who I'm convinced was Edward Snowden, because the main wall in the second bedroom was covered floor to ceiling in mounted computer monitors.

The kitchen ceiling has caved in twice. Whenever there's a hurricane, rain comes in through the living room windows. There's one outlet in my room and eight in the kitchen. The windows all face the same direction—into the alley—so there's no direct sunlight. Hot water is an elusive third roommate, and there's no water pressure, so when you shower you have to push the soap from your body with your wet hands. I've seen a mouse come in through an open window. I've woken up with a cockroach on my face.

And yet it's home. It's *my* squalor. I've spent over a third of my life here. I've had over a dozen roommates—a fellow writer who would pick all the carrots out of her vegetable soup; a gay finance guy who ironed his ties every night; a straight actor who would stand shirtless in my bedroom doorway and play with the hair around his nipples while asking me about my day; and a scenic carpenter who must've been palm-sanding his girlfriend's vagina, because I could hear her moans from all the way down the hall.

I once heard my next-door neighbor cough through my bedroom wall. It was so clear and pronounced that it was as if he were in the room with me. I froze where I sat, positively mortified, because if I could hear him cough, he most *certainly* could hear my gay porn and whistle tones, and had been hearing them for years. No wonder he never says hello to me in the hallway.

I have two female neighbors across the alley—our apartments

directly face each other—and I hate them. They're always sitting out on their fire escape smoking and clucking like fucking hens until all hours of the night. I fantasize about the fire escape coming loose from the building—not entirely, but just enough to scare them. During the winter months they hang, smoking and squawking, out of their living room window like half-inflated air men in front of a car dealership. One night, they pulled the window up so forcefully that it fell out of its frame and shattered on them with a loud crash. Like, the glass broke on their huddled bodies, and the frame fell around their waists like a hula hoop. They were fine, but they still screamed and screamed, and, watching from my couch, I laughed and laughed.

There's a classical pianist across the hall. Every afternoon and early evening he plays, and it's magical. Sometimes he'll have a violinist over, and I'll cross my fingers that it's love.

The only neighbor I know even slightly is the woman down the hall. She's in her early fifties, maybe, with rapidly graying hair and, for many years, a sweet little shih tzu. The three of us always wound up in the elevator together, and I'd shove my Pottery Barn catalogs and rejection letters under my arm and bend down to pet the dog. Over the years the dog became slower and less excitable, and then my neighbor started carrying her into the elevator, and now my neighbor just gets in alone.

My building is situated on the busiest stretch in the neighborhood, above a family chiropractor and a barbershop that's open until 2 a.m. and serves a glass of merlot with your fade—full-bodied and velvety, with notes of your own hair. On my block alone there are three Chinese restaurants, two that are fine and one that will give you the shits; a diner where the waitresses run out in the middle of taking your order to hug their friends on the street; and a bodega run by a sweet Asian family where the Fruity Pebbles are up so high you have to call out for help getting them, and the owner's son won't move to help you because he'd have to step off the milk crate he stands on behind the register in order to look tall for the women he flirts with in line.

In front of the bodega sit two homeless men, one of whom is a disabled Vietnam vet and another who several times through-out the years got clean and on his feet and then fell back again. People in the neighborhood interact with them frequently, bringing them things from the bodega. One morning on my walk to the subway the woman ahead of me stopped in front of the disabled vet, swooped down, and grabbed his cane.

"You don't need this," I heard her say to him. "You can fuck-ing walk. You don't need this."

He grabbed the cane as well and shouted, "Leave me alone!"

"You can walk, you piece of shit—I know you can walk," she said, pulling him to his feet with the cane. "That's right, get up!" she continued. "Fight me for it!"

"Fuck you, bitch!" he screamed back at her, obviously not in any shape to fight her.

A man ran out of the bodega and separated them, telling the woman, "Walk away, just walk away."

"You're defending a rapist!" she said to him.

"I didn't rape nobody!" the homeless man shouted.

"You're defending him," the woman continued. "You're a piece of shit, too."

"Walk away," the man said steadily.

"You piece of shit."

"Please, just walk away."

Finally she did, and I retreated into the subway station, rattled beyond belief.

On weekends Jehovah's Witnesses somehow get into the building, and they go from apartment to apartment trying to save souls. Usually I ignore them or say "No, thank you!" through the door, but one Sunday afternoon some friends and I were heading to Ikea to buy runners (so perhaps we deserved it) and we opened the door to three ladies holding an array of pamphlets.

"I'm going to save you some time," my friend said. "We're all homosexuals headed to Ikea."

The women looked at one another. The one closest to me rifled through her pamphlets, handed me one with several robed disciples on it entitled *Biblical Attire*, and said, "Well, here's something about fashion."

The neighborhood is one-third Dominican, one-third Orthodox Jewish, and one-third musicians and singers of varying success levels. I've blown most of them, which sounds like promiscuity, but in the right light it's community organizing. It's a great thing to do if you love real estate and comparing apartments, which I do, and I hope to one day suck an eight in a classic six.

In the building across the street from mine, for example, the closeted college student who came in my eye has built-in bookshelves[1] and a live-in super.[2] One avenue block east, I was admiring a tightlipped chef's south-facing windows[3] when he pulled me to the floor and put his foot to my neck, and I noticed his floorboards warped in every corner.[4] In an art deco building ten blocks north, a baby product blogger with a sunken living room[5] and *two bathrooms*[6] but no elevator[7] greeted me at the door with a kiss and a mint julep.[8] His living room was crowded with strollers sent to him by manufacturers for his review. He picked me up, kicked them every which way, and carried me to his bed. I deeply enjoyed being carried, and almost asked if he had any BabyBjörn samples lying around that I could be strapped into and brought places.

There's a beautiful cluster of Tudor-style co-ops a few blocks north of me that I'd *love* to blow someone in, just to see the interiors. The courtyards are straight out of a romantic comedy, with paved paths and manicured swirls of green grass and old-timey lamps hanging from stone arches—you can just see Rachel McAdams getting spun around in there. Those apartments used to have a full view of the Hudson River until high-rise condos went up right in front of them, completely obstructing their view. I have blown somebody in there—an Indian surgeon with a high-floor apartment that overlooked the George Washington

---

1 Great for displaying your Margaret Atwoods, knickknacks, pictures of friends and the people they married.
2 He/she has a stake in the building's upkeep, as it is also his/her home.
3 Best direction for sunlight, casting aspersions, etc.
4 A bad contract job if I ever saw one.
5 Helps differentiate energy zones.
6 Exciting guest soap opportunities.
7 A nightmare.
8 We'd never met before, but why not?

Bridge and nether regions that smelled like Andes mints. He opened the door, and I ran right to his terrace. It turns out that worry, like cold air, doesn't rise, and I stood, feeling peaceful, looking out at the Hudson and the bridge and the West Side Highway roaring directly beneath. After ten polite minutes he cleared his throat and asked, "Shall we get to it?"—rightfully worried that he'd invited over a total stranger who would never leave his terrace.

On a handful of summer nights I'd get out of the subway one stop early in order to climb three steep, not-built-to-code flights of stairs up to the apartment of a man from Georgia—"The country, not your state," he said in his thick accent. He had a massive collection of Virgin Mary figurines in his living room, enough to fill two hutches and a windowsill. He'd sit on a folding chair in front of them and place a roll of paper towels at his feet for when we finished. One time I was bold enough to lean up and kiss him, and he kissed me back hungrily, biting my lip so hard it bled. The living room was the only room in his apartment I ever saw, but one time I could hear the faint sound of clothes tumbling in a dryer and thought, *He's so fucked-up, but he has laundry in the apartment!*

I have yet to hook up with anyone in my building, but god knows I keep my eyes peeled. There's a skater boy whose center of gravity I imagine is quite good, but he doesn't even hold the elevator door for me. I watched my hot neighbor across the airshaft put up curtains. We recently got a laundry room in the basement, which would be the perfect place for a New York meet-cute. Imagine it: the night frigid but the laundry room warm, Bruce Springsteen's "Human Touch" playing softly on a nearby radio, and a few of my delicates mixed in with the neighbor's firefighting gear. "Are these yours?" he'd ask. "Sorry, it's so hard to wash out rescued children's grateful tears. Want me to run those through again for you?"

Then, back in his apartment, in between frenzied, passionate kisses, I'd say, "Talk dirty to me: Are these doors solid- or hollow-core?"

Go Together Like a Horse and Carriage

I love weddings. I love a string quartet; I love the bride's and groom's parents; I love a kindly, nonthreatening officiant. I love the vows. I love how nicely everyone cleans up, I love a seated dinner, I love an open bar. I love going dark for thirty minutes with a glass of Prosecco on the terrace, if there's one at the venue, and then I love going light again when they play "This Will Be (An Everlasting Love)," or "I'm Coming Out," or any song from a yogurt commercial, really.

Do I want to get married? Sure; I mean, I haven't really given much thought as to what I'd want—the Plaza, a hundred fifty people, the Reverend Joan Didion—but yeah, why not, maybe.

OkCupid claims that Massachusetts has a higher concentration of matches for me than any other state in the country. So when I had to go to Boston for a cousin's wedding, my eyes were peeled.

The T ride out to Harvard was full of bespectacled men with hair flecked blond from playing Frisbee in the sun. Along Brattle Street the V-neck-bedecked men in the coffee shops were reading *The Economist* and sipping black coffee. There was a young man walking his bike with a textbook under his arm that I may or may not have followed for a couple of blocks in the hopes of somehow getting ahead of him and throwing myself under the wheels of his bike.

The rehearsal dinner was a sea of young button-downed Harvard men from legacy families. My mother, one beer in, started waving at me from across the room and pointing at men she thought were gay. I'd report to her later that I saw her "picks" out on the deck canoodling with women, to which she'd scoff, "It's a ruse!"

I hate the Lower East Side and normally avoid it like the plague it's most likely festering with, but the other night I went. The streets teemed with really skinny people in leggings pouting and posing. Walk one block down Rivington and tell me it's not just a bunch of collarbones smoking. On every street corner there'll be some guy leaning against the side of a building looking pissed, or some girl with one leg up on a fire hydrant, actually pissing.

At the end of the night, while I waited for the westward subway to rescue me, a drunken straight couple stumbled up to me. "Can you be a witness?" the woman asked. She got down on one knee and said to the man, "I want you to fucking marry me, you fucking fuck."

Her beau politely declined, slurring out, "You don't have a ring."

She took her hair band out and began tying it, along with several long stray hairs, around his ring finger.

"Now will you fucking marry me?" she demanded.

He nodded: he would. They looked at me.

"Congratulations," I said.

Their eyes narrowed, suspicious of me for being less drunk than them.

A train pulled into the station. "Woohoo!" the woman shouted, and threw herself against the closed subway doors, falling back down onto the platform. Then she got up and, with a grand sense of occasion, licked the length of her new fiancé's face.

I was at a beautiful rehearsal dinner in the Napa Valley. It was one hundred and eight degrees, and we all held our gin and tonics to our necks. Family and close friends spoke, and then maybe thirty-five minutes into it, the groom's cousin got up. She took the microphone and said, "This is a bittersweet occasion for me. Sweet because it's a wedding, but mostly bitter."

There were titters in the crowd. We thought, *Oh great, a sardonic cousin, she's got a really great, dry joke coming*, but then she continued, "For all my life I've been trying to get Adam to fall in love with me. And now that he's met the lovely Stacey, I can see that's not going to happen!"

She took the air out of the room. Which was impressive, because we were outside.

Usually at wedding receptions I'm seated at the adult version of the kids' table. You know, the table by the door, or the one next to where the band eats their shift meal. It's the seating chart equivalent of that pile of unique, lone socks from the laundry—

awkward cousins, beloved college professors, single friends who took the Bolt Bus up.

At the wedding of two good friends in the Berkshires, I was seated next to the groom's cousin and her fiancé: Tara and Ken, as I came to know them. "I haven't seen James in, like, eight years," Tara said, eagerly grabbing the vodka-cranberry Ken promptly brought her and taking a gulp. "But family's family. We all show up." She took another gulp and turned to Ken. "I can already tell you I'd like another."

"You want one?" he asked me. He had an endearing aw-shucks grin.

"Sure," I said, and he high-fived me.

When he returned with another round we cheers'd, and I asked them how long they'd been together.

"Eight years, on and off," Ken said.

Tara added, "I was a fucking idiot and kept breaking up with him."

"I waited. Each time." Again he grinned. "I knew you'd be back."

"I came to my senses."

"Nah," he said, "I just got you drunk."

She raised her glass to him. "That, too." He laughed and clinked his glass against hers.

"Have you set a date?" I asked.

"Next summer, we think," she said. "We just want to go to Mexico, get married on the beach, drink margaritas, hear music at night, ride bikes—"

"Mark my words: she will not get on a bike," Ken said to me. "Her drunk ass falls off every bike I've seen her on."

"When?!" she demanded.

"Myrtle Beach, Patterson Park. You face-planted in Cancun, and that girl put it on YouTube." He downed his drink and turned to me. "Another?"

We were already three rounds in and dinner had yet to be served, so I said, "I think I might need a breather."

"No," he said. "No!"

Tara leaned in. "There are no *breathers*."

I nodded okay, and off he went. I turned to Tara. "You guys are good together," I said.

Her face twisted, and she looked at the seat he'd just vacated. "I loved him before I even fucking met him," she said. "And when I did, it was like, oh, *there* you are."

Ken was back a moment later. "They're putting out fried chicken," he said, setting our drinks down on the table.

Tipsy and moony, I clasped my hands together like Jessica Tandy and asked, "How did you propose?"

They looked at each other. "Like, a year ago, maybe?" Ken said. "We were in a bar—"

"It was a drunken dare," Tara clarified. "I dared you to propose."

"I'd been wanting to," he started, and she cut him off.

"But you were so scared to ask me!"

"Well, I didn't know whether you wanted to!"

"What did you do for a ring?" I asked.

"I curled, like, a plastic straw," he said. "You know, like, the red straw that comes in, like, a gin and tonic—"

"Gin and tonic, vodka-soda," she added. "I've got a real ring now, obviously." She leaned forward, showing me.

Ken chewed on the ice in his drink, grinning proudly. "Dirty girl goes good," he said.

She slapped at him playfully, and he looked at her before he laughed. I noticed that his eyes scanned her constantly for approval. If he made a joke and she didn't laugh at it, I could tell he would instantly apologize. He wanted nothing more than to make her laugh, bring her drinks, marry her if she dared him to. He adored her and would do anything for her, and she knew it and cared for and deeply valued him. They were hot messes, but they were funny, and they dared to be together. I loved them. Best kids' table ever.

At the rehearsal dinner for another cousin's wedding in rural Ohio, my aunt and uncle asked all the attendees to write down on an index card a Recipe for a Good Marriage, something like "Schedule a regular date night," or "Don't go to bed angry." My mother, the divorce lawyer, wrote: "Keep your finances separate."

I didn't know what to write, so I didn't write anything. What do I know about marriage? A friend once said to me, "Marriage is not getting to leave after."

So maybe I should've written that: "Don't leave after."

Things I Know to Be True

- - - - - - -

If you use the lint roller just right, it can feel like physical affection.

If you close your eyes, all the people around you playing Candy Crush with the volume up will make you feel like you're in *Amélie*.

If you say nothing to him, you could still say anything to him.

Any therapist worth his or her salt will have candy out at Halloween. Trick or treat! You have emotional problems.

To exercise portion control, crush the remainder of a bag of tortilla chips to crumbs, eat half a pint of ice cream and spray the rest with Raid, and throw ham out the window.

"Thanks, man." = "We will not be making love."

If you drink enough pink wine, a whole new section of YouTube unlocks for you.

Don't suck dick to The Smiths.

If you get a low balance alert from your bank, before you assume your identity was stolen, first make sure your identity isn't just that of someone who's terrible with money.

Phone sex is only good with sociopaths. Go on, get purred at by someone who's been removed from a will.

Sometimes when you're taking yourself to dinner, the restaurant will seat you by the coats, and people who are leaving will smile and nod at you as though you are part of the restaurant. Just smile and nod back.

Ten p.m. = vodka midnight

If you can hear your fart above your music, then everybody else can, too.

Youth groups in Starbucks = thirty caramel ribbon crunch Frappuccinos for thirty Madisons and Jadens

Pursuing actors is ill-advised; if you run out of saliva, you can rehydrate, but what happens when you run out of praise?

Indoors > Outdoors

Hell is other people chewing.

Daylight only adds to porn. So do tattoos—there's nothing like a frat guy with three fingers in his ass and Psalm 23 on his chest.

Ohio: just a bunch of structures to get murdered behind.

If you want to endear yourself to doctors, keep interrupting them with: "Really? Because I read somewhere . . ."

The urge to not even try is always the closest, the handsomest.

Don't forget that once you've finished eye-straddling and eye-riding the man across from you on public transit, he'll want nothing to do with his eye-child.

Go to parties and talk about pollen. True friend material will respond.

A Curse

To the girl who sat next to me on the subway last night: you kicked and elbowed me several times while trying to cuddle, nuzzle, and get all up on your boyfriend, and you did not apologize or even seem to notice.

I curse you like the gay spinster witch I am.

When you have sex—when you squeeze him so tight and try to force your two bodies to become one, a devil-may-care process you started on the subway in my personal space—may your sweaty chests begin to make that awful farting sound. You know how when two chest cavities are sliding against each other it sometimes sounds like a juicy fart? May your lovemaking produce that sound.

May you unsuccessfully try to laugh it off. May the sound become so unavoidable that you feel him racing to finish in order to stop hearing it.

Afterward may you both sit with bowls of stale Frosted Flakes, watching *House* on Hulu in total silence, and may you feel farther away from him than ever before.

The Law Student

I never should have grabbed his dick.

It seemed like a good idea at the time; we'd watched a Laura Linney movie and had sushi. But it was not a good idea at the time, that immediately became apparent, and I let go of his dick like it was an item I could not afford in a store I thought I had a coupon for.

Let me back up.

The dick I grabbed belonged to a sweet and handsome guy I'd met through my blog who'd just moved to Brooklyn to go to law school and wrote to me asking for a date. He didn't know anyone in New York yet and I knew with each passing day he'd start to meet people in New York and acquire perspective, and perspective is the enemy, so I acted fast. Two nights later, we sat under the Brooklyn Bridge and ate ice cream and talked for three hours. This was right after the 2008 Democratic primary, and he'd campaigned hard for Hillary—met her, even. He lost his mother and brother to cancer within the span of a couple of years, and now he and his dad were learning to get by, to rely on each other. He had an *Into the Woods* lyric tattooed in Sanskrit on his left calf. At the end of the date I told him I'd had a really nice time, and, his face lifting with relief, he said, "Really?" He'd been nervous.

On our second date he held the door of a subpar vegan restaurant for me. On our third he came to my apartment, tossed me onto my bed, lifted me to him, and kissed me. On our fourth date, at his place deep in Brooklyn's nether regions, we ordered said sushi and watched said Laura Linney movie and got into bed. We began to kiss, and as we did I slid my hand down inside his underwear and around his penis.

"Whoa," he said.

"What's wrong?" I asked.

"It's just—I'm from Indiana."

I yanked my hand away. "Too fast?" I answered for him. "Too fast."

"I'm sorry."

"No, don't be sorry!" *You filthy slut*, I cursed at myself, *you thought you could have your cock and eat it, too. This boy is from Indiana and he loves musicals and our American criminal justice system and he reaches for door handles for you, and you, what do you reach for?*

We didn't touch for the rest of the night. We just slept, and when I awoke in the morning I was startled to find him standing in the doorway, his phone in his hands.

"My best friend just called me," he said. "She woke up and some strange guy was asleep on her couch."

"*What?*" I asked.

"Yeah, he got in somehow in the night, and he was drunk and passed out on the couch."

"Oh my god, what did she do?"

"She got him to leave, finally. He was still pretty fucked-up. She's really freaked out. I told her I'd call her back."

"Jesus. That's so scary. Thank god he didn't hurt her."

"Yeah." He shifted in place. "So I told her I'd call her back."

"Okay, yeah, good."

"I don't want to be rude and call in front of you."

"Oh, no, that's okay. Do what you need to do."

"No, I mean, I'm probably going to be a while, so . . ." He drummed his fingers once on the doorframe. "Like, don't feel like you need to stay here if you need to get going."

If a giant vaudeville hook could've yanked me out of the scene, it would have. I'm surprised the Sandman wasn't sent in. "Okay! Of course! I should head home anyway!" I said, springing into action and, of course, dropping everything I tried to put on. He handed me my socks.

I kissed him good-bye, and his lips were like a sea wall against my affection surge. As I walked to the subway for my two-hour commute home, I thought, *Wait a second—did he just make all of that up to get me out of his apartment?* I once leaped out of bed at 6 a.m., telling the painter, sleep-talker, and cover hog next to me that I simply had to write, turned on all the lights in my room, and began to loudly type into a blank Word document (DOO-DOO-DOO, WORKING) until he sat up and said, "Well, I guess I should leave you to it," just so I could get three solid hours of me-sleep.

A few days later I got the "it's not you, it's me, I just don't know where my life is going" text, and I don't know about you, but I really think it's time we retire that line. It bores me to tears.

If you're going to dump me, at least take me by surprise. Here are some alternative options—I'm just spitballing here:

"I went to see my grandmother on her deathbed, and her dying wish was that I stop seeing you."

"I'm afraid of you."

"I'm starting a new religion, and you're our Satan."

I still think about him. I think about his kindness, his propriety, his good, wounded heart. He seemed like someone who could teach me something, give me perspective, get me out of my head. He was a nice guy, he was good, and I was excited about him. I was excited that someone like him could be excited about someone like me.

I never should have grabbed that dick.

Love Poem for the Preppy Guy with the Single Cupcake

- - - - - - -

To which skinny bitch
are you bringing home that cupcake?

Will she be curled on the couch
watching *Rizzoli & Isles*,
her hair pulled tightly into a ponytail,
showered and sipping a glass of red wine in her Yale T-shirt?

Will her teeth be blue
from the wine
and her eyes dead
from the Connecticut?

Will she put your cupcake on a plate
and scrape the icing off of it
like an extreme home makeover?
Will she break off bites of the cake between two fingers
and deliver them to her mouth halfheartedly?

Will she whine,
"It's too much, I'm faaaaat,"
and then show you pictures
of a high school friend's wedding
on Facebook?

I would never put your cupcake on a plate.
I'd eat it right out of the bag.
I'd probably even eat a little *of* the bag,
if it proved to be an obstacle.

Cooking for One

- - - - - - -

- *Grilled Four-Cheese Sandwich* -

WHAT YOU'LL NEED

4 hard cheeses
4 hard truths
Sourdough bread

Casual Sex Correspondence

To the gentleman on Manhunt who wrote:

> *thanks for your kind words, but unfortunately your profile is too sex-focused. kind of a turn-off. sorry*

This site's called Manhunt. Upworthy's down the hall. Make a left.

To the gentleman who pointed directly at me on the street and hissed, "*Grindr!*":

Was I just Hester Prynne'd?

To the gentleman on Manhunt who wrote:

> *LOL you faggot troll, you cock goblin, you're gross, get off Manhunt.*

With "faggot troll" I will take issue, but "cock goblin"? Hats off. If only all the unrepentant assholes I meet on the Internet could have such rich folkloric imaginations. It's a shame you weren't working for Jim Henson in the glory days. How vivid, how vibrant: the cock goblin.

Goblins are evil, yes, which, fine, I'll cop to—a couple of times I've closed my eyes on the subway and pretended to be asleep when someone needed a seat. It is difficult to distinguish between a male and female goblin, and, you know, if a blind-folded stranger sat next to me during *Fried Green Tomatoes*, they'd be hard-pressed. Goblins hold grudges—I do have a one-strike policy for eating chili over books I loan you.

But! Goblins are also fiercely devoted to anyone who befriends them, anyone who takes the time to try to create an understanding. This devotion is never-ending, and when their loved ones perish, goblins are said to weep at their graves.

Who'll weep at yours? Look, my goblin eyes are dry.

To the gentleman who made me hide in his closet so he could pay his cleaning lady:

First of all, she totally saw me. Second, that's all you pay her?

How to Build a Fire
(in Thirty Easy Steps)

- - - - - - -

1. Have a glass of wine.

2. Put on a grandfather sweater, something heavy and seafaring that lands at the hip, with a nice cable knit and dangly sleeves and little candies in the pockets that you can discover later.

3. You are about to build a fucking *fire*. Take that in. Text as many people as you can to tell them about it. Alert social media.

4. Get on iTunes and make a fire-building playlist. Careful not to go too brooding; this isn't a funeral pyre. You want melancholy/reassuring. Minor chords that yearn for the major. Guitar. People who sound like they have beards. Women of the woods. Women of Ireland. Places where the sea beats at the rocky shores and goats sleep in the house.

5. Why isn't anyone texting you back? Text more people.

6. Visually assess the situation in the fireplace. There'll probably be a lot of really disgusting charred stuff—gross. Use the big metal chopsticks to push all that off to the side.

7. Open the flue?

8. Crumple up four pages of *The New York Times*, preferably a favorable review of your nemesis's play, and lay them down. Your first layer. Refill your wine in celebration.

9. Place on top of the crumpled newspaper a grid of kindling. Kindling is any piece of wood the size of an Olsen twin. The grid, you've been told, is key. It allows oxygen to flow from the burning favorable review of that jackoff's play to the actual logs on top or something, you don't know, it all seems really complicated and maybe not worth it, maybe you should just quit while you're, oh, thank god, someone's texted you back; well, now that a sufficient quorum of attention has been acquired, you have to proceed.

10. You're ready for a big log. Are you *ever*. Laugh sardonically out loud as you place the big log on top of the grid. That's right, laugh *to yourself*, because who cares? You are fabulous company.

11. Light a match. Promptly blow it out and make sure you have the best possible song playing for when you light your very own fucking *fire*. Sit at the computer for a minimum of fifteen minutes responding to e-mails and picking out the right song. For this moment you'll want more of a streak of weathered optimism, a driving beat pushing things forward—but not celebratory, not joyriding; you want driving as in a bittersweet ride through the neighborhood you grew up in, during which the passage of time and the inevitability of age is fully felt. Driving like that.

12. Light another match and drop it dramatically like Susan Sarandon onto the logs.

13. Light another match and drop it maybe not so dramatically this time, maybe like Dame Judi Dench, onto the logs.

14. Light another match and, you know what, just kneel and light the newspaper directly.

15. Run screaming away from it.

16. My god, it's enormous. The flames are so huge! The fire is crackling and spitting at you. The two of you aren't exactly hitting it off, so try to ease the tension with some topics of general interest. (For example, you both enjoy oxygen.)

17. Have just a *teensy* bit more wine and maybe a candy from the pocket of your old salty man sweater.

18. Take a phone call, commiserate briefly about that favorable review in the *Times*, then tell your friend you have to go, you're very sorry, but you simply must sit by the fire and be fiery.

19. Long for a wingback chair, and for your book to write itself. Laugh ruefully. *Yes*, a rueful laugh goes great with a fire. Do it again.

20. Watch that favorable review wither into a bouquet of hot orange-black curls, and kick yourself for not having more hurtful things to burn.

21. Remember that that would require opening up and letting someone get close enough to you to hurt you every once in a while. Decide that an accumulation of hurt is indicative of, for better or worse, a life lived to the fullest, and that therefore your life is empty. Pity you can't burn that realization.

22. Can't you? Try anyway.

23. (You can't.)

24. Open another bottle of firewine and finish off the last—wine becomes less something around heat—you read that somewhere at some point—so you'd better just do that thing with it that we talked about.

25. Give some thought to the man who cut this wood. Imagine him clearly, a shock of handsome Americana in the woods, fur against fir. The ax an extension of him, the wood splitting happily for him. His name Carter or Caleb. No, Anson. *Anson.* His rough hand in yours at the movies. Not that he goes in for movies all that much, but he knows you like them, and he puts on a clean shirt for it.

26. Think about how fabulous it would be, while fighting with Anson, to smash your wineglass on the fireplace, or throw your wine *onto* the fire, causing it to roar in agreement with whatever you're saying, perhaps something like, "I married *you*, Anson, I didn't marry the woods!"

27. Put on some Robyn. Time for a mood change. Dance a little. Get pagan. Get Dionysian. Let the fire inform you, compel you toward a new level of being. Alert social media to your new level of being.

28. At this point the smoke detectors will go off and the room will be full of smoke. Scream. Open the windows, open the door. Scream a whole bunch. I cannot convey to you how important it is to scream your head off at this point. You might even want to alert social media to the danger you're in.

29. It's quiet now, the smoke detector sated by your screams and the fresh air. Feel properly chastened. Who are you

to think you can build a fire? Run to iTunes and make sure you have the right song playing for sitting and feeling chastened.

30. Due to your cellar being full of firewine and your emotional cellar being empty of hurt, feeling chastened will lead only to arousal. Lie back and close your eyes, choke slightly on the traces of smoke still in the air, let a hand travel the length of your old-man-and-the-sea sweater, and let your thoughts return, again, to Anson.

The Hockey Player

I have met my fair share of characters through Match.com. There was the filmmaker who showed me his incomprehensible short film and, when I asked a thematic question, said, "It sounds like you just didn't get it." There was the guy who pronounced guacamole "guacaMOHLAY" with hipster flourish when he ordered it. There was the theater director who after dinner took me to Gracie Mansion, handed me a copy of Lorca's *Sonnets of Dark Love*, instructed me to "read softly," and, as I did, gently tossed seashells from a Ziploc bag one by one into the East River. It was Lorca's birthday, you see, so.

And then there was the Hockey Player. Yes, a real live hockey player.

After several chats online and on the phone—during which I grew impossibly excited by his deep voice, his thick Brooklyn accent, and his total ignorance of the fine arts—we agreed to meet in my neighborhood for dinner, steps from my apartment and, more importantly, my bedroom. I knew that on the off chance a queeny nerd and a retired minor-league hockey player didn't have much to talk about, there would be the language all men speak: the filthy brogue of our dangling need.

He arrived at the restaurant even better-looking than in his pictures but wearing an extra-extra large Islanders jersey. I reached out for his hand, but he slapped it away. "None of that handshake stuff," he said, and scooped me into a bear hug. My feet left the ground. "Nice to fuckin' meet ya."

"Are you hungry?" I asked, adjusting my cardigan and catching my breath.

"Nah, I ate already."

I paused. "But we were going to have dinner."

"Well, I'm still gonna be drinking," he said.

When we sat down in the restaurant he blew out the candle on the table. "Fuckin' dangerous," he said.

When the waitress came to take our order, he told her, "I went to the doctor today. It's not lookin' good."

"Oh no," she said.

"Yeah," he continued, "he's got me on a special liquid diet. Nothing but beer. Keep 'em comin'." She stared at him until he clarified, "I'm jokin', sweetheart."

We made conversation over my turkey burger and his six beers. "So, you write the lines and people say them?" he asked. "That's awesome."

"It's okay," I allowed, and he insisted, "No, don't fuckin' undersell it, it's awesome," making eye contact.

"Well, I couldn't play ice hockey," I started, and he took a swig from his beer, laughed, and said, "I would fuckin' love to see you playing ice hockey. You and your little glasses. Trying to protect yourself."

The waitress came by. He ordered another beer and I got a martini—why not? I liked the way my shoulders still hurt from his bear hug. He told me he'd taken a total of six pucks to the head.

"Fuck yeah, they hurt," he said. "That's vulcanized rubber just attacking your face. I've been knocked out cold, just dead on my back, like, a hundred times. None of my teeth are real. They made me a new cheek. My head's been just fuckin' open on the ice."

Having finished my martini, I reached forward and touched the scar on his hairline. He leaned into my touch.

"And that's not even counting the fights," he said.

Apparently, in ice hockey, even though everyone's wearing a huge helmet and face gear, it is still possible to give someone "the wrong kind of look," which causes everyone to "pile on."

"I fuckin' bit a guy in the eye," the Hockey Player told me.

He'd been hit in the ear, he said, and was told he'd suffered hearing loss, but he was skeptical. I was not; he had hearing loss. Case in point: "Why did you retire?" I asked him, and he answered, "I did some shopping and played video games, what did you do?"

"WHY DID YOU RETIRE?" I repeated.

"Too many surgeries," he said. "I'm strung up like fuckin' Pinocchio here." Then he smiled a little: "Aw, fuck. Sorry to be goin' on and on about this. I know it's not all arty or whatever."

I asked him if he missed it. He stared at his beer and said, "Every fuckin' day," and I swear to god, it looked like he was going to cry. "All this beer," he finally said. "Gotta piss. Little boys' room."

When he was in the bathroom the waitress brought me the check. "In case you're ready to *leave*," she said, with extra emphasis.

I was looking at it when the Hockey Player returned to the table. "What? Don't touch that. What, are you crazy? I got this. I got this," he said.

"Oh, you don't have to do that," I started, and he cut me off.

"I asked you to dinner," he said with startling command. "Let me fuckin' buy it for you. I want to."

I tried to imagine myself sitting in the stands with the other hockey wives, enjoying Karen's Rice Krispie Treats and getting a group together to go to Josh Groban. I could see it. So I went to bed with him.

Can I just tell you—two words: Nordic corn-fed. Soft white-blond hair everywhere, pale skin, and muscles inherited from the pillaging-rapist generations that came before him. My sheets smelled like pale ale when he left.

A few days later he called me. He was in his car, driving into the city. "I'm about to go tie one on before I go to this stupid dinner," he said.

"What dinner?" I asked.

"Just some friends I went to fuckin' high school with. So how are you doing?"

"Oh, I'm all right," I said. "I'm at work, though, so I can't really talk right—"

"What is with this woman's haircut?" he muttered, and then I heard him shout, "*Hey lady! Billie Jean King called, and she wants her fuckin' hair back!*" I had to hold the phone away from my ear. Back on the phone, he was now laughing. "Hoooo, she did not like that very much. She just gave me the double bird. So, anyway, what've you been up to?"

I stepped away from my desk and put a finger to my other ear. "I'm sorry—did you just shout that at some woman on the street?"

"Yeah, she had a fuckin' ugly mullet," he said.

"Well, that wasn't very nice of you."

"Yeah, what can I say? Fuck. I don't want to go to this dinner. That's why I'm drinking tonight. What time do you get out of work?"

I heard honks and sirens in the background, sounds that I could now only imagine he was actively causing. "At seven," I told him.

"Oh, I was gonna ask if you wanted to get a drink."

"Maybe another night. You could come over or something."

"We'll see what the beer tells me to do," he replied. "What the fuck is this guy doing? *Use your fucking turn signal, asshole!* God, I hate driving in New York. One of these days I'm just going to ram into a bunch of cars."

"Please don't do that," I said.

"Sometimes I feel like it."

"I know," I scrambled together, "but that won't make you feel better."

He softened. "You're always so sweet. Let me call you later. After this fuckin' dinner and I've had a few drinks."

Later that night, in my bed, I asked how dinner was.

"Fuckin' awful," he said. "They didn't like how much I was drinking. They didn't like that I smoked."

"Well, maybe they were just concerned for you," I said, thumbing a circle on his stomach.

"I said to them, 'If any of you have a problem with me, get up from this table and take it outside.'"

My jaw dropped. "Oh my god," I said.

"Yeah. And none of 'em fuckin' stood up. None of 'em."

"I don't think they wanted to *fight* you," I said, sitting up.

He sat up as well. "And you know what that makes them? A bunch of pussies."

"But they're your friends!"

Leaning in to kiss me, he whispered, "Fuck 'em. They're pussies."

Even though he continued to contact me, I never saw the Hockey Player again. After a while he moved to Rhode Island and became a state trooper. He lasted a week on the job. I know this because he called me, drunk, and told me that he'd been fired and was being sued by—well, by Rhode Island.

You see, the only thing worse than a hockey player with an aggression problem is a state trooper with an aggression problem. The facts were these: he'd pulled a man over for speeding. The man was belligerent and, after a heated exchange with my Hockey Player, took a swing at him. The Hockey Player took him down, choked him on the side of the highway, and crushed his windpipe, sending the man to the hospital.

The Hockey Player was fired, taken to court, and ordered to go to therapy. His therapist was alarmed by his aggression problem—apparently it's one for the books. He was sent to specialists and finally diagnosed with Huntington's Disease.

Huntington's is a degenerative brain disease, and, according to the drunk, sobbing Hockey Player on the other end of the phone call, he had two years to live.

It's been suggested to me that this could all be untrue, but I don't know. He continued to call me, maybe once every couple of months or so, always late at night, always drunk, sometimes with a lot to say and sometimes with nothing; he'd just ask me about my day, tell me to just talk, and I'd hear him breathing with effort—and this carried on for the better part of a year, until it all stopped.

The Lonely Christmas Poem

It's a few nights before Christmas,

and all through the house,

not a creature is stirring,

not even a mouse,

because it died on your dishes.

It's a few nights before Christmas,

and all through the house,

not a creature is stirring,

not even a louse,

because you've blown everyone in northern Manhattan.

And parts of Fort Lee.

Not a telephone is ringing,

not a text message is dinging,

because your friends are all sound asleep in bed,

in their homes—homes they purchased

with their own money—
sleeping next to mates—mates they attracted
with their own strengths of character.

They didn't used to have money;
they didn't used to have character.

When and where were *those* acquired?

Some even have children.

You care for your Facebook statuses like children.
You dress them, smooth their hair, and send them out into
    the world,
hope that they're well-liked.
You do the best you can with them.

It's a lonely Christmas.

It's a few nights before Christmas,
and all through the house,
not a creature is stirring,
not even the four Girls Golden,
who skip and stutter on the television,
the back of the DVD
cracked from codependence.

Not a porn star is moaning,
not a porn star is groaning,

they simply looked through the screen
directly at you
and, exasperated, whimpered,
"Again?"

Your therapist has urged you not to watch porn
and instead rely on your imagination,
which, for the record,
is not the place it used to be.

Not a drunk person is falling,
not a *Twilight* fan is bawling;
seventy-two hours of video are uploaded to YouTube
every minute
and you've watched all of them.

You've reached the end of the Internet,
a place you've heard of only in fables,
but you're there,
and it's a game of spoons with Ann Coulter.

It's a lonely Christmas.

It's so quiet.
There's a cheese for that.

The box of wine perches on the refrigerator amiably,
its spout a shrugged suggestion:
Have some. Have some!

Not a creature is stirring,
except for you.
You stir.

And then so suddenly
to your mind come the things you wished for
when you were growing up:
fame, fortune, Felicity's boyfriend Ben.
It was only when you had those things
that it would all begin to matter.

But it has always mattered,
despite your plans and preparedness.

You make a list for now,
a list of wishes:
a new vacuum cleaner,
groceries,
a salt-and-pepper DILF
in robin's egg shorts,
peace in the Middle East
and trenchmouth for people who make out in public,
a cure for AIDS
and an Oscar for Annette Bening,
true harm to no one
and Ryan Gosling for everyone,
funding for arts education
and, well, just education in general,
cynicism for the optimists

and sentiment for the bitches,
paradise for those who have passed
and more time for those who have not,
eczema for the vain,
a seat on the subway,
trust that time, in addition to succumbing you further
to illness and loss,
has a parallel ability to ripen you further,
and a mandatory six months in food service
for every man, woman, and child.

Also you wish for love without any work.
Love where nothing changes.

With each passing year you find it harder and harder
to reveal yourself to men.

You wish for love without any risk.

Which is gutless.

But to your list you add it anyway.
Because there is comfort in a list of wishes,
in words on top of words,
stacked like the apartments
just outside your window.
One or two are still lit from within,
still awake with you
deep in the night.

Try It

I was on the subway on my way to work one morning when a youngish, long-haired man in an argyle sweater came skipping onto the train. He skipped up and down the car, singing to himself, until he stopped right in the middle, swung on a pole, and said, "Hello, friends!"

The fuck out of here was everyone's silent response.

"Look around you!" he cooed. "Look at all of this diversity!"

He swung on the pole again, giggling.

"I mean, think about it: Who on earth are you sitting next to?" he asked. "Good question—it's *good* for you. Who is on Earth, and who is next to you? Wouldn't you like to know? You can. All you have to do is look up. Look up! There are people all around you, people you can know. Try it!"

He turned to a middle-aged woman.

"Hello," he said to her.

"Hello," she said back, smiling despite her better efforts.

"That went well!" he said. "That could've gone way worse! Try saying it to the man next to you."

Several of us around her met eyes and smiled, our interest piqued. A teenage girl took out her earbuds—a feat. The woman obediently turned to the man next to her, and quickly said, "Hello."

"Hi," the man said.

"Look at that!" the youngish man proclaimed, and promptly burst into tears.

He knelt and began to talk about Jesus. The teenage girl put her earbuds back in, the newly acquainted man and woman went back to their respective *Post* and *Daily News*, I snuck out a fart, and the day pretty much proceeded in ordinary fashion after that.

Box Office Hall of Shame

‑ ‑ ‑ ‑ ‑ ‑ ‑

Here, culled from over a decade of customer service, are my top ten worst, most loathsome customers:

10. The woman who asked, "In light of the bad reviews, you're still charging full price? Well, *ha*, that just doesn't seem right."

9. The man who said, "You're lucky there's glass between us, princess."

I mean, I *was* dressed for the ball, but still.

8. The woman who asked, "Are you giving away any free tickets for tonight? My daughter's in the show, and it just pains me to have to pay to see her when I get to see her for free every other hour of the day."

"Oh," I said. "No, we're not."

"*Fine*," she snapped. "But she'd better thank me."

7. The woman who screamed, "I'm going to get you fired! I'll write to your boss, and you're gonna be out of a fucking job! I'm going to write to *The New York Times*!"

"Lady," I wanted to say, "I've been trying to get my name in the *Times* for years."

6. The woman who sobbed, "I can't come tomorrow night because I booked a gig! I'm a pavement-pounder. I have to work! It's my livelihood! You want me to sacrifice my *livelihood*?"

"Well, each sale is final," I tried to explain, "but maybe there's someone you could give the ticket to, or sell it to?"

"*No!*" she shouted. "The only person I can think of who'd like this show is me!"

5. The woman who couldn't bear the four minutes she'd had to wait in line and barged to the front, slammed her hand on my windowsill, and said, "*Excuse* me, I am a trustee of this theater, and I will gladly *pay* for these people's tickets if it will get you to *move* this line a-*long*."

4. The woman who showed up forty-five minutes late and said, "Well, I think I should only have to pay half of the ticket price, since you're only letting me see half of the show."

"Ma'am, you missed both of our late seating breaks because of how late you were," I said. "If you'd like to come to another show and see it from the beginning, we have a policy called past-dating—"

"Okay, do you want to hear *my* policy?" she sneered. "My policy is you, oh, I don't know, maybe try to be a *human being*."

We had her e-mail address on file, so I went home and signed her up for a bunch of e-mail spam. Enjoy the INSANE PUSSY SQUIRTING VIDS!!!, ma'am.

3. The woman who calls us every season, claiming she's on our mailing list and demanding to be removed. We can never find her in our system, and this angers her. "You're all faggots and whores!" she screams. "You all slept with Mike Bloomberg to get your fucking jobs! You were part of 9/11!"

Like I said, this happens every season. She's our Santa Claus.

2. The woman who chased people through the lobby waving cash at them, trying to get them to sell her a ticket. When I told her to cut it out, she shouted, "You're racist!" She wound up getting a ticket, but ignored the assigned location and sat in the center of the front row, which was being held for a group of disabled veterans. "Fuck that," she said. "If they were coming, they'd be here by now."

She's also the reason several downtown theaters no longer have public opening-night parties—she would get in the buffet line, pull empty Tupperware containers out of her backpack, and fill them with food.

1. The husband and wife who were on the waiting list for a sold-out performance and went to dinner, ignoring the time we asked them to be back, so when they weren't present we sold the tickets to the next people on the list. "We are very busy people," the wife yelled. "We do not have time for this. How *dare* you skip us?"

"We called your name, and you weren't here; we had to proceed," I said.

"I don't want to speak to you any further," she said. "You have an attitude that I am against"—she put her hand to her heart—"*spiritually*."

"Those are the rules."

"I feel sorry for you—you and your rules," she continued. "You know who else loved rules? The Nazis. You'd better be careful; if I didn't know any better, I'd say you were acting like one of them!"

Good thing she knew better and didn't say it.

Ails

- - - - - - -

For a while I went to a dentist on West End Avenue, where I saw a sassy Latina sparkplug hygienist named Carmen. I loved her, but she was eventually fired for trying to sell skincare products to all of the patients on the side.

"So, tell me everything," she'd always say, numbing my gums and starting in with the hooks. "What's going on in your life? Who's loving you?"

"Ohnnnwouh," I'd answer.

"Why is no one loving you?" she asked during one of our final checkups.

"Ooodellmee. Ihwomwomovingoo?"

"Oh, yes," she said, wiping the blood from my chin. "He's a currency trader in Chicago. He's moving here. Open wide, please. He's so handsome and tall; he looks like a basketball player, and I look like his stripper girlfriend."

"Atsfast!"

"Gargle and spit." She clicked her nails together while I did as I was told. "He's moving here for work, not for me. I do not move fast. My mother always said, 'Things that start fast end fast.' I'm sad no one's loving you."

"I exchanged numbers with someone last week, but I was so nervous I think I might've sucked all the romance out of the inquiry. Like your little tube that sucks up my blood, just—"

She tugged on my lips with her gloved fingers, poking around in my mouth. "Still bloody. Gargle again. Why are you nervous?"

"He's out of my league. He's a premed ex-Mormon! He's on a real life journey. What am I, a WASP with gingivitis?"

She stopped and looked me dead in the eye. "You don't have gingivitis. Don't joke about that." In she went with another hook. "And no one's out of your league, honey."

I started to smile, and that's when she added, "I can give you something for the chin acne, you know."

"You have one of the worst necks I've seen in a long time," the chiropractor said to me. I laughed, and he said, "It's not funny.

"First let me show you an ideal neck," he continued, and popped an X-ray into the machine, which in turn projected for me the neck of, I assume, someone with a balanced checkbook and a bleached anus. "See?"

I nodded with what I hoped was the desired amount of reverence, but then began to worry that because of my horrible neck I also nodded horribly. I watched myself nod in his mirror, and I looked like Katharine Hepburn.

"Now look," the chiropractor intoned gravely, and laid on top of the ideal neck another X-ray. "This is *your* neck."

I gasped.

"I know," he said.

My neck looks like it saw the ideal neck coming and crossed the street to avoid it: *Oh no, it's the ideal neck. I can't deal with him today, I'm just out running errands.* My neck sets out like Columbus for a brave new world, making an obedient *Pinta* and *Santa Maria* out of each of my shoulders. My neck forgoes college for backpacking across Europe and playing its music, only to prodigal-son its way back home and enroll quietly at the community college at the top of my back.

This all started a week or so earlier—I was about three-quarters of the way through masturbating (let's say eighty-five minutes in) when I began to get a shooting pain in my chest and arm. I switched to a looser grip, but the pain did not subside. *Am I dying?* I thought. *I'd better hurry up, finish, and address this.*

Once I'd finished, my arm and chest throbbed yet again with pain. *I'm dying,* I thought. *It's finally happened: I've jerked myself to death.* I sat in my chair, frozen. I went online to look up the symptoms of a heart attack and promptly began to suffer from all of them. The Internet tells you explicitly that if you think you are having a heart attack, you should *not* try to convince yourself that you aren't—you should instead go immediately to a hospital. Unfortunately this requires surrendering something to which I hold fast: caring what people think about me. On the fifty-fifty chance that it was a false alarm, I could just picture the intake nurses glaring at me, thinking, *I took a break from pacing the hospital, obsessing over my workplace love triangle, to come deal with this drama queen?*

I crawled into bed, sweaty and nauseated, and thought to myself, *You've had a good life; you saw the Pacific Ocean, you had some plays up, men of varying repute held you in their arms.*

I thankfully woke up in the morning, but my back and neck were stiff as boards and it hurt to move. "Oh my god," one of my coworkers said, "you have to go to a chiropractor. Go see mine."

"Are you listening to me?" her chiropractor now repeated. "Your neck is terrible."

"*Terrible?*" I repeated, not wanting to be glib, but merely trying to place this on the scale of widely accepted terrible things—was it, like, war-terrible or PDA-terrible?

"Yes, terrible. What are you doing that could've caused this?"

I rattled off likely factors—I'm a stomach sleeper, I'm aggressively inactive, I have the posture of someone who's constantly trying to disappear into himself—while the likeliest factor seemed inherently clear to both of us: my years of running in my mouth and throat a halfway house for troubled cock.

"This affects not just your whole body but your whole mindset," the chiropractor continued. "I wouldn't be surprised if the headaches and the lethargy and the depression were caused by this misalignment."

I didn't recall telling him I was depressed, but no matter. He called my attention to a chart of the human spine on his wall. Listed at each vertebra were things like "anger," "fear of change," and "deep old hurt," or, as I know them, Tuesday. I looked at the bottom of his chart: © 1978.

"Get changed back into your clothes and meet me out at the tables," the chiropractor said. "We're going to help you."

"Great," I said, relieved.

"We're going to straighten you out," he declared, and then flexed his arms and growled, "*In more ways than one.*"

"Ha, okay," I said, trying to be agreeable, and then thought, *Wait, what?*

"Have I ever told you the story about my client who took human growth hormones?" the guy cutting my hair asked me.

"No," I said, not wanting to remind him that this was the first time he'd ever cut my hair. "You haven't."

"This was maybe ten years ago," he said, starting in, snipping my hair away at key moments. "This guy was so beautiful (*snip*). He had dark hair, he had clear skin (*snip*), he had ice-blue eyes like a vampire (*snip*)."

"Nice."

"At first he told me he was an underwear model, but then he told me he was an escort. And he made *money*. He was always going to Brazil or Barcelona with some guy and making ten thousand dollars." He switched scissors. "And I don't make judgments. However people want to live their life is fine by me. He had an eight-pack. I was, like, drooling into his hair as I cut it. Shorter on the sides?"

"Yes, please."

"God, your hair just grows and grows."

"It's the hormones," I said.

He stopped and swiveled my chair to face him directly. "Are you taking them?" he asked gravely.

"No," I said, terribly sorry.

"Oh, thank god." He swiveled me back. "One of the last times

I saw the guy, I was telling him to stop taking them, and he says to me, 'I don't think about tomorrow, I think about today,' and I said, 'You are hurting your body,' and he was very mean to me. I realized that he had probably just taken a shot of hormones, because you turn evil after you've had a shot. He came back later and apologized. He said he was going on a three-month cruise with a bunch of other escorts. They'd been hired by some businessmen to sail around the Baltic Sea and just have orgies with everyone on board. They were each getting paid, like, fifty grand."

"Jesus," I said.

The stylist nodded and sighed. "I didn't see him again for years. And then—get this," he added, leaning in. "He came in a month ago."

"No."

"*Yes*. He said to me, 'Oh, you're still here.' I said, 'Where would I go?' I didn't even recognize him. He'd lost his hair. His teeth were brown. He was wearing a long-sleeved shirt, and this was a guy who wore a skimpy T-shirt even in the dead of winter." He shook his head and buzzed around my ears. "He said he was having kidney problems. One of his balls just shriveled up and disappeared."

"Oh, god," I said. "Okay, that's enough detail."

"After he left I just went in the back and cried. He said he didn't think about tomorrow, but I wanted to say, honey, it's tomorrow. Tomorrow is today." He shook his head again and ran a comb through my hair. "How's the length on top?"

I stood in an examining room at the free clinic on West One Hundredth Street, my pants and underwear around my ankles, in front of a squat, sour Asian female doctor. I held my limp penis, she held a Q-tip, and we stared at opposite walls. I was young. I was young and impressionable—so impressionable that I'd had gonorrhea impressed upon my penis by the throat of a fast-talking biology major at Vassar who was in New York for a summer internship.

I was mortified. "I think you gave me gonorrhea," I texted him.

"Really?" he wrote back. "I feel fine. Sure it wasn't someone else?"

I could hear the doctor's jaw tighten, her salivary glands rouse. She was waiting for me to produce some of the itching, burning discharge I'd complained of so she could send it off to the lab, but whatever sample-sized patience she walked in with had dwindled.

"It will hurt less if I don't have to go in for it," she said—truly one of the most horrifying statements I've ever heard, although what she said next was *the* most horrifying. "Pump it."

"What?" I asked.

"Your penis. Pump it."

Was she . . . ?

"Pump it," she repeated.

I began to, well, pump it.

"Pump it from the base," she commanded.

I pumped it from the base. This was officially the most humiliating moment of my life, and I once accidentally squirted balsamic vinegar onto a man's foot at a buffet. Finally a little discharge emerged, and she swabbed it and made her exit.

I was given an antibiotic smoothie concoction that tasted like cement, and a few days later it was confirmed that I had indeed had gonorrhea, or, as I call it, an honorary degree from Vassar.

Obit for a Murse

- - - - - - -

A man's purse, known collegially and on the street as a "murse," passed away in early spring of this year. The black, two-handled murse was four and a half years old, a longer-than-average lifespan for murses, so its death was not unexpected. It went peacefully, splitting open from the bottom at its home in New York City.

The murse was born in Japan, or perhaps in Taiwan, wherever Uniqlo manufactures its murses. The murse was purchased and lovingly owned, and is survived, by Isaac Oliver, who continues to live in New York City and carry needlessly voluminous bags around.

The murse enjoyed many days dangling from the limp wrist or sloped, ineffectual shoulder of its owner, as well as evenings spent tucked under theater seats or standing out like a sore thumb in gay bars. It often contained a cell phone, Listerine strips, the same book for months at a time, travel-sized Eucerin, bodega receipts, and, only once, a giant water bug. It was great on trips—it happily held up to three folded cardigans. Keys once fell out of it onto East Thirty-Eighth Street, a disappearance that went undetected and led to a day of multiple horrors.

One favorite memory, shared by the owner: at Marina Abramović's exhibition at the Museum of Modern Art, there was a doorway in which a nude man and woman stood, facing each other, and the only way to gain successful passage was to turn to one side, face one of them quite intimately, and maneuver through. The murse's owner faced the woman because he wanted to feel a man behind him (the owner has insisted we print that he does not regret the choice), and as he emerged from the doorway the murse caught on the two naked bodies behind him, and they had to raise their arms and angle their bodies differently so it could be pulled through. "Sorry! My murse," the owner tried to explain to them, but they remained stone-faced, committed in the way that only volunteers can be.

Funeral services will be held at the waste bins in front of the St. Regis Hotel on East Fifty-Fifth Street. Reception and thirty-dollar martinis to follow at the King Cole Bar, where the murse once proudly occupied its very own stool, creeping everyone out.

Subway Diary

- - - - - - -

A train, 1:00 a.m., Sunday

A drunk man stumbles up to my friend Dave and me and says to us, "Don't sit like that." We ignore him, but he persists. "Don't sit like that," he repeats. "Stop it, don't sit like that."

Our legs are crossed, which doesn't necessarily mean you're gay—Dave, for instance, is straight until he's taken an Ambien—but this man is not interested in nuance.

He stands right over us. "Stop it," he says one last time, and finally reaches down, grabs my knee, and pulls my right leg off my left. Then, somewhat abated, he stumbles off.

N train, 12:30 p.m., Saturday

The girl sitting next to me gets a text message. I read it over her shoulder. It says: "Let me lick your clit until it cries tears."

A train, 8:00 p.m., Wednesday

At 125th Street a young woman jogs slowly up and down the length of the car, a bottle of soda in her hand. "Outta my way, motherfucker," she mutters. "Outta my way."

People let her through, except for one woman who gets elbowed.

"Outta my way, you stupid bitch," the young woman mutters. "You're a stupid bitch. Outta my way."

She elbows a man.

"What are you, retarded?" she mutters. "Outta my way."

Everybody presses up against the sides of the car to allow her a clear path on which to run back and forth.

"What are you, retarded?" she repeats. "Outta my way. Stupid bitch. I'll fuck you up. I'll fuck you up. Everybody lookin' at me. What's wrong with you? What's wrong with you? What are you, retarded?"

The man sitting next to me extends his legs and blocks her path with his feet. She stops, but she does not look up. "Outta my way," she mutters.

"Stephanie," he says, calmly.

"Outta my way."

"Stephanie."

It's silent; then, finally: "Yes?"

"Chill out, Stephanie," he says. "You know me. You know who I am?"

"Yes."

"You know who I am?"

"Yeah, I know who you are."

"So stop it. Leave everybody alone, Stephanie. Nobody's doing anything to you. You leave everybody alone now."

"Okay," she says. "You're right. Okay. You right."

"Are you all right?" he asks her.

"Yeah, I'm all right," she answers.

He stands up and touches her shoulder. "Why don't you sit down?"

"Okay, you right. You right." She sits. "Everybody's lookin' at me."

"Nobody's looking at you," he says.

"Like there's something wrong with me. What's wrong with *them*?"

"Just chill."

"Open this." She hands him a bottle of soda. "She won't stop looking at me."

"You're fine," the man says.

"I'll beat her ass."

"You're fine. Nothing's wrong." He hands her the soda, and she drinks it. His cell phone falls out of his jacket pocket, and he reaches down to pick it up.

"Old-ass phone," she says. "What are you doing with that old-ass phone? Get a new one." She laughs.

He laughs, too. "Yeah, it is a pretty old phone, isn't it."

"Yeah."

Over the Knee

Every couple of months or so, a scruffy young Italian guy in my neighborhood will come over and spank me. He travels a lot, but whenever he's in town he'll hit me up. He works in the music industry in some capacity, although I doubt it's artistic, since the downbeat eludes him.

It started as a normal hookup, with him grabbing my ears and shoving me down on him one placid Sunday afternoon. *Castaway* was playing on his television, and I tried to ignore it, having not yet seen it myself! Things were going well, and his hand traveled down my back and cupped my posterior.

"What a fat ass," he said, which is not really something you want to hear in the line of duty, but his tone was appreciative.

"Thanks," I said, "I'm mostly sedentary."

He rubbed it a little and then raised his hand high and brought it down hard onto my right cheek. *Whack!* I nearly bit his dick off. I sat back, my body charged. We stared at each other.

"Too much?" he asked.

Too *much*? I'm the son of a preacher; I went to church twice every Sunday. I turned the other cheek. He yanked down my jeans, ripped off my underwear, and slapped me (*whack!*) so hard (*whack!*) across the bare behind (*whack!*) that had I pearls, I would've clutched them.

"That was fun," he said after, walking me to the door.

"Yeah," I replied.

"Let me know if it hurts to sit," he said, a roguish twinkle in his eye.

Through the years we've stayed in touch. "You look good," I said to him once, having not seen him for maybe six months, and he did—he'd lost some weight and changed his hair.

"You painted," he said another time, nodding toward my bedroom wall as he kicked off his shoes.

"Oh, yeah," I replied, taking one last gulp of water. "I needed a change from the red."

I always get the urge to call him immediately after I've gone on a date with someone nice. Like the assistant publicist who bemoaned Glenn Close's Oscar-less state to me in a wine bar and then tried to hold my hand as we crossed Forty-Second Street. (*Whack!*) Or the folk band manager who made a Google doc of restaurants he could take me to, shared it with me, and gave me editing rights. (*Whack!*) Or the arts educator who, naked in my bed, looked up at me and said, "I'm kind of new to all of this, so forgive me." (*Whack!*) Forgive him. (*Whack!*) Nice guys, all of them. (*Whack!*) What the fuck.

Inside of me there is a wall, over which a handful of men have thrown stones or hit whiffle balls, and they are never heard from again. My therapist at the time, perhaps thrilled to talk about something other than the television shows I'm watching, jumped on this. "The tables are turned with these guys," he said.

"They like you. They're opening themselves to you. Is it hard to think of yourself as the one capable of hurt, as someone who could inflict pain?" I told him if he kept up that level of real talk, he could find himself a new Wednesday ten thirty.

A few evenings later I was yet again over the music guy's knee. As he throttled away, I stopped and thought, *Well, wait a second. This guy's funny, he's successful, he's dominant, he's away a lot—why not try?* I grabbed his raised hand at the wrist and pivoted around and up to kiss him squarely on the mouth, something we'd never done. I could taste his spearmint gum. He pulled away, smiled politely, and pushed me back down onto my stomach.

Texts from My Parents
on Their Cruise

- - - - - - -

From Mom:

we r on ship there is a friends of Dorothy mtg im thinking of going 2

From Dad:

Isaac we are on ship mom on her first daiquiri I bought a hawaiian shirt love dad

Attend This Tale of Icy Gays

- - - - - - -

I was in San Diego for a weeklong box office software conference (you read that right), and my coworker and roommate for the conference swore to me that not only would there be gay guys in attendance, there'd be *tons* of them. "Really?" I asked. "At a box office conference?"

"Oh, yeah, totally," he said.

And sure enough, on the first night, as the all-volunteer choir sang the box office software company's mission statement in funereal five-part a cappella harmony, I glanced around the ballroom and saw a sea of primped and plucked lookers in plaid. Here I'd thought I could spend the week coasting, maybe witness a couple of open-bar-induced dustups between undersocialized IT people, but no. I looked down at my own plaid button-down, wrinkled from the suitcase, and thought, *My god, they all ironed their clothes in their rooms. It's going to be that kind of conference.*

A night or two later, after I'd grown hip to the ironing and the fact that the bok choy at each meal was not an endless Southern California bounty but the previous meal's bok choy in a heavier canola glaze, there was a picnic dinner at a marina park on San Diego Bay. It was a beautiful night. Scraping the sky around us was one shiny-tacky luxury hotel after another—the tumescence of the '90s. Again there was an open bar, but no nerds were throwing down. My coworker found me and told me he'd met a group of guys at a mixer one of them threw in his room the night before—really, a gay mixer at a box office software conference, twelve queens in a two-queen room at the Grand Hyatt—and that I should meet them, too.

As we approached their table I could see the five of them, lips pursed, heads cocked, eyebrows raised, their vodka-sodas sweating rings onto the table. We were outside, so the fog machine and Rihanna were implied.

Arriving at their table, my coworker introduced me. Their eyes rolled up to meet mine. "Heeey," they murmured in unison, and brought their drinks to their mouths, as if to make clear that their lips unpursed for me only because they needed another sip. I reached out and offered my hand to the first boy on my left. It took him ten whole seconds to raise his hand and limply shake mine, and that's when I decided that I was for sure going around the table and forcing them all to shake my hand. One by one, each slowly lifted his hand to mine, wrists up and fingers dangling, as if I'd stumbled upon the world's meanest puppet show.

My coworker pulled up two chairs, and we joined them at the table. "Where's everybody from?" I asked.

They each mumbled where they were from, except for the one to my immediate right, who simply lifted his name tag so I could read it for myself if I wanted to know so fucking badly. And then—here's where it got really good—no one said anything else. We just sat there, in total silence, for a good four or five minutes.

"They're really nice, I promise. They were just being weird," my coworker insisted, but it was too late. Those guys are Icy Gays. *Icy Gays.* Icy Gays are the worst kind of gay people, narrowly beating out Political Bottoms. You can tell you're in the presence of Icy Gays if there's a chill in the air and a hiss in the consonants and you suddenly feel like you're inadequate in every possible way. They're gay Slytherins. Beware.

"They've rented a boat and are going out on it tonight," my coworker told me another night. "They invited us. Me and you." I told him I had no intention of getting on a boat with them; an iceberg would undoubtedly crash into the boat, trying to hug its brothers.

On the last night of the conference there was a big blowout dinner on the USS *Midway*, where an all-volunteer band played pop songs with box office software–specific lyrics ("Rolling in the Deep" became "Putting Butts in Seats"; remind me to sing it for you sometime), and there was once again an open bar—an open bar on a vessel, and still no nerds were throwing down. I shook my fist at the bay and had five drinks. My coworker found me and drunkenly proclaimed, "I did it! I melted the Icy Gays! They were awful, but I melted them!"

I congratulated him and headed back to the hotel, where I was delighted to hear that a drunken database administrator had been escorted to her room by hotel security after jumping on several men and peeing herself in the lobby.

Anyway, it turns out that the Icy Gays were nicer with lots of liquor in them. They warmed. Which makes sense: an Icy Gay is merely an Awkward Gay who got the pomade to work right. And they can try to deny it as much as possible and ignore those of us who still struggle daily with our hair, but it'll always be clear, at least to me.

Dance as fast as you can, fuckers. I can taste your tears in mine.

Cooking for One

- *Arroz con Pollo* -

WHAT YOU'LL NEED

2 chicken legs, w/o skin and rubbed with salt and pepper

1–2 tablespoons olive oil

1 text to local gay, craven

½ an onion, chopped

1–2 tears, because of the onions and hard truths

1 text back from local gay, equally craven

1 trash can for all of the above

Big Ben

"d o you miss my dick?" the text read.

My thumbs hovered above my phone. Miss Manners didn't set any sort of precedent for this situation, so I responded as casually as I could: "Who is this?"

"It's ben," he replied. "I used to live on Bleecker and Lafayette. Live in London now but back for business on the 28th."

"Ben," I wrote back, "I most urgently miss your dick."

Ben was a web programmer I'd met online a year prior. *Masculine, often scruffy, and big-meated*, his profile read. *I'm a friendly guy and live my life traveling. I'm open-minded and a little cray in the good way. Into espresso, pyramids, octopi, traveling, lions, sushi, crystals, deserts, oceans, forests, dicking.*

I'd spent an evening with him in his studio that looked like a cell. He shaved and did dishes at the same sink. His refrigerator had a bottle of ketchup and a lime in it. The room glowed a constant dim green from the codes of data scrolling up his computer screen. Terrifying, but he looked like Ashton Kutcher, and what could possibly drive someone that attractive to be a serial killer? So I stayed.

I've been on the business end of a lot of dicks, so I've seen what the rest of us got, and Ben got *the* dick—a pink, girthy eight you could slam a door with. If I could be holding that dick right now as I write this, I would. I want my Christmas card to be a photo of that dick and me in matching sweaters. I want to hit the road and see America with that dick. I want, in old age, to look up from my needlepoint and see that dick doing a crossword, trying to stay sharp for the grandkids.

Another text from him popped up, and I ducked into a Starbucks to read it. He wrote: "ur mouth is like my dicks camp friend. reunion on the 28th?"

The man could turn a phrase, and his sexts were commanding, as though he had two licked fingers inside every phrase he sent. His imagery was inventive, his syntax surprising, his structures parallel—if the University of Iowa Writers' Workshop ever offers an MFA in Dirty Talk, I can recommend a department head. He sent me photos of him with his dick out on the London tube, at a movie theater, in a restaurant bathroom. I sent him only one photo, from the privacy of my own bedroom, which I'm sure will surface in some way after this book has been published. (Although, by now that photo's been in so many American homes it's basically a Getty image.)

And then he wrote, "Cant wait to cum in your ass."

I wrote back, "Sorry to quibble, but you mean you'll cum in the condom, right?"

"No, in your ass," he responded.

"Sorry," I wrote, "I only play safe."

"I'm negative."

"So am I. Still."

He began to type in lowercase. "i just don't know if i can keep it up in a condom. i hate the smell. it's like a medical scene. i get completely turned off."

"I won't do it without a condom," I wrote back.

Again, lowercase, and now missing punctuation: "we can try it w/ a condom but i dont think itll work out as well i want to show you what its like to really be fucked"

Over the next few days we didn't correspond. My phone sat still and quiet. I thought about him nonstop. *I mean, we've already hooked up. What's the worst that can happen? If I was going to catch something from him, I would've already caught it.* Then: *No, no, no.*

On the twenty-eighth, at two thirty in the morning, Ben texted: "come over"

I watched the phone, inert.

Again it buzzed: "please? you up?"

I'd stayed up, hoping he would text, and now he had. What was I thinking? *Turn your phone off and go to bed.*

Buzz: "you there? i need u so bad"

I picked up the phone, texted back: "I'm up, but I'm nervous after our last conversation."

"itll be good"

"It has to be safe," I texted.

"ok - take a cab - ill give you $ for it"

I stood, still fully dressed from the day, and paced my room. Even if he had safe sex with me, he'd probably had unsafe sex with other people, and who knows with what frequency and to what extent?

My phone buzzed with another text: "I want to be with you."

The capital "I," the "be" "with" and "you" all full words, the period at the end—it was the first time that formed sentence and I had ever crossed paths, and I took off toward it. I walked out of my building and an empty cab pulled right up, complicit, as if my bad ideas employed a doorman. *What are you doing, what are you doing, what are you doing*, each rotation of the car's wheels seemed to thump at me. It only made my dick throb.

We embraced in the doorway of his hotel room, and he kissed my neck and told me I smelled nice. I thanked him and didn't tell him I was wearing a sample of Sarah Jessica Parker Lovely that I'd gotten from my mom. He picked up a wad of cash from the bedside table and handed it to me, and of *course* it had to have been on the bedside table, he couldn't have picked that up from any other flat surface in the room, but I pocketed it nonetheless.

He brushed his teeth while I channel-surfed. We spooned and watched MSNBC. When he reached for his phone to quickly call a colleague in London, I saw that magnificent penis tenting his boxer shorts, and I heard music.

I grabbed it and put him in my mouth, and his voice in tandem trembled. He finished the call and put both hands on my head. Twenty minutes later he began to grunt and buck, so I pulled away and began to jerk him off. This is when he groaned and said, "What is it going to take to get you to swallow my cum?"

"I prefer to watch a guy come," I said. "I think that's much hotter."

"Oh, come on."

"Sorry." How strange to continue jerking someone off after saying sorry.

And then he said, "So this is what twenty-seven dollars gets me."

I let go of his penis, which landed against his stomach with a thud. "Excuse me?"

"What? I'm just kidding."

"You offered me that money to help me out with a cab so I could come down here in the middle of the night."

"Don't be like that," he said.

"Like what? That was a really shitty thing to say."

"I was really close, and then you stopped because you're scared or whatever. Come on, don't stop."

I shook my head and stared at the floor.

"Forget it," he said finally. "Fuck this." He pulled the sheet up to his chin. "I don't get you," he continued. "You're so fucking weird. You're so cold and distant in bed. It's like I'm with a prostitute or something; it's like you have a condom in your mouth that you're gonna roll on my dick when I'm not looking, because you don't even want to be near me."

"Whoa," I said, "I'm sorry, but I was actually having fun until two minutes ago."

"I don't think you were," he replied. "I could've gotten an escort, I could've picked up a guy in a bar, but no. I wanted to be with you. I wanted you here."

"Well, gee, thanks."

He propped himself up on an elbow. "I mean, my god, are you *that* scared of AIDS that you don't even want to have sex with someone?" he asked.

"Well, I don't think having sex and being at risk for AIDS is the same thing, exactly," I said, and he cut me off: "You don't trust me."

"What does that have to do with anything?"

"If you trusted me, you wouldn't have pulled away."

"Do *you* trust me?"

"Yeah, I do!"

"How can you trust me?" I asked. "You don't know anything about me."

"It's a gut feeling," he said. "I know immediately if I trust someone."

"That's not trust—that's instinct. Those are two completely different things."

"I disagree."

"Trust requires time and evidence," I said.

He flopped back down onto his back and covered his face. "What a horrible way to treat people; like they have AIDS or something."

"I just have limits for what I'll do," I said.

He removed his hands from his face and looked right at me. "That's an awful way to live."

I stood. "Okay, I'm going to go." I stumbled around, trying to find my clothes.

"At least I respect people," I heard him say.

He was trying to hurt me, and he was succeeding. "I respect people," I said.

"I highly doubt that."

Is this my underwear? Yes. *There's one sock.* Where's the other?

"You make me feel like shit," he said.

"Well, I'm sorry. That was not my intention." *Shirt on.* Pants clocked behind the easy chair.

He was on his feet now, too. "What are you going to do, get a cab?"

"I guess," I said.

"I mean, your cab could crash on your way home and you could die, but what are you going to do, not take the cab? Live your life in fear of that? You can't control it."

"Oh my god, that is so not the same situation."

"You can buckle your seat belt, but that won't save you."

"Actually, it *will*," I said, tying my shoes.

"Whatever, man." And then he stood between the door and me. "You shouldn't hook up with people if you're this scared."

"Maybe you're right," I said.

He didn't move. "I mean, why the fuck are you doing this?"

"I don't know," I said.

"What the fuck do you think you're doing?"

"I don't know!"

"Why the *FUCK*—"

"I DON'T KNOW!"

His eyes flared open, wide and angry, and he reared back. I slammed my eyes shut and braced myself, because oh my god, he was going to hit me.

But he didn't. Instead it got quiet. I opened my eyes, and his face, still beautiful, was now crumpled like a child's. He looked down at his naked body, covered it with his hands, and crawled back into bed. I would rather he had hit me.

I pulled his money from my pocket and put it back on the bedside table. "Good night," I said.

As I left the room he shouted, "I guess I'll just jerk off now and let my gross, horrible cum out where it'll catch AIDS!"

I cried on the street and in the cab. Outside the window the East River unfurled like a shock of dark cut glass. I'd circled the entire perimeter of Manhattan in one evening. *Why the fuck* are *you doing this?* I thought to myself, and tried to answer. Because I want to. Because I'm lonely. Because I'm still in formation. Because sometimes it feels good. Because it's good practice for when it counts.

Practice—the word felt loud in my head, as if this was all some dress rehearsal for a life that would begin in informed earnest shortly, once the fates were ready. But no, I was living, and the men all counted, and everything I was doing counted, and this was my life—tearing away from a volatile stranger's hotel room at four thirty in the morning in a cab I couldn't afford.

A little while ago I saw Ben online again, with updated photos and a new profile with a new username. *In Motion* was his headline, and inside he wrote:

I'm usually very to myself but I like to open up from time to time. We're all bisexual trannies using an alien body to experience a holographic illusion. How's that for being a normal masc bro?

I don't know why I did it, but I wrote "hey" and sent it.

"hey," he responded.

"How's it going?" I wrote, clicking through his photos. He was standing in an art gallery in one of them, a crowd of people milling behind him, and he was lowering his pants and flashing his cock.

"if this is who i think it is," he wrote back finally, "i'm sorry."

I paused. "It is," I responded. "And thanks. I am, too."

"Still in the Heights? Still writing?"

"Yes, and yes. I'm working on a book, actually."

"Rad."

"Still in London? Still programming webs?"

"Beijing now. But I'm in New York currently. Near you, actually."

"Really?"

"Yep. Do you miss my dick?"

Scene from a Box Office

ELDERLY MAN: The last two shows I've been to at your
theater I have not been able to hear one word out of the
actors' mouths! Not one iota. At your most recent production I was in the second row, and even though I'm
sure the author didn't write a mystery, it was a mystery
to me.

ISAAC: I'm very sorry, sir.

ELDERLY MAN: I went and got tested out on Long Island,
where they do tests on people, and I'm completely gone
in my left ear, but my right's still got a little zing. They're
gonna give me my very own device. So my question to
you is: I have a ticket for next week—can you switch me
to a date next month when I'll have my own device and
I can hear it?

ISAAC: Well, sure, let me see—

ELDERLY MAN: Oh, please, sir! I love Shakespeare. I've
seen everything; even back during the war I would go
and see plays, back in '44. What did I see in '44? Eh, it's
all gone. One ticket is all I need. My wife hates it; she

won't go. She hates the language. I don't know why—
she's always talking herself. Do you have anything at a
matinee? My wife worries less if I'm at a matinee. She
thinks things will happen to me out in the world, and
she may be right.

ISAAC: Could you do the first Wednesday matinee in
April?

ELDERLY MAN: I'll take it! Thank you; you've made an
old man very happy.

ISAAC: Well, of course, I want you to be able to hear it!

ELDERLY MAN: I can fake my political meetings, but I
can't fake the theater; I need to hear it. You don't know
this yet, but it's horrible to get old. It's the worst thing.
You want to scream and shout, but your arms don't move.

Love Poem for the
Hot Young Dad Holding
the Newborn on the Subway

- - - - - - -

Lose the wife,
lose the kid,
keep the swaddling blanket,
let's do this.

Judged

- - - - - - -

I'd always wondered who watched *The Big Bang Theory*, and I got my answer bright and early one fall morning in the jury selection room at the federal courthouse for the southern district of New York in downtown Manhattan. They'd asked us to list the television shows we watched and passed a microphone around.

"*The Big Bang Theory.*"

"*Big Bang, Scandal, Grey's.*"

"*The Big Bang Theory, Scandal, Good Wife.*"

"*The Good Wife! Big Bang Theory! A little Breaking Bad!*"

When the microphone came to me, I said, "I mainly rewatch a bunch of shows that aren't on anymore, like *The Golden Girls* and *The Comeback* and *30 Rock*, just over and over again?" and at that point I'd lost the room.

"I'm surprised I'm the only one willing to admit this, but I'm not ashamed," a woman a few rows ahead of me declared into the microphone, her voice a piercing, nasal goose honk. "I watch all the *Real Housewives*. I can't get enough!" I craned my neck to get a better look at her. All I could see was hair, and lots of it, piled like cinnamon buns on top of her head. Her denim jacket had Wile E. Coyote embroidered on the back, holding up a small handwritten sign ("Help!").

Next they asked us where we got our news. I went full liberal: "Um, just NPR and *The New York Times* and *The New Yorker*," which is a total lie, because all *The New Yorker* does is pile up and scare me, but I ended with, "and Gawker and Facebook," in the hope that I would sound indiscreet. I could see both the prosecution and the defense scribbling notes, and I prayed they were writing *Gossipy gay: dismiss.*

"I get all my news from my husband!" Denim Debbie announced, the microphone back in her hands. "I don't read a thing. He tells me what I need to know!"

I tried to recall the very encouraging welcome video they showed us downstairs in the main holding area, in which Sandra Day O'Connor talked about civic duty, the right to a fair trial, and the importance of everybody's participation in this process. "Wouldn't *you* want you on your jury?" she asked. I wouldn't want me on my jury—a few nights earlier, instead of going to a real restaurant alone, I drank a margarita in Chipotle by the bathroom, so I was in no place to be judging anyone—but I got picked nonetheless.

"Isaac Oliver," the judge's head clerk called out, "Juror number seven," effectively taking away my name and giving me a new one.

I climbed into the jury box, trying to take it all as a compliment. More people were called forth by name and assigned juror numbers—#8, #9, #10, #11—and, finally, as Juror #12, they called her. They called Denim Debbie. She leaped from her seat and ran to the jury box, smiling and waving at us excitedly; you would've thought she'd been invited down on *The Price Is Right.*

As she climbed into the jury box, I saw her head-on, and she was all hair, heaving mouth, and hungry eyes that churned with an almost atomic energy. They stopped on me, and we made prolonged eye contact as she climbed up to the row behind me. It was basically the beginning of a Western.

The rest of the pool was dismissed, and we were sent to the adjoining jury room for a small break. The jury room was small and straightforward—a room with a big table in it—but we were on the fourteenth floor, and the large windows gifted us with a stunning northerly view. We all stretched and exchanged beleaguered smiles. The mood was bleak. You couldn't shake the feeling that we'd all done something wrong.

"I can't wait to get to know all of you!" Denim Debbie goose-honked. "Are we allowed to get to know each other?"

"Hopefully we won't be here that long," an older woman replied, tossing a pashmina over her shoulder and almost hitting the guy next to her.

A few of us sat around the table, and others went to the windows and looked out.

"Well, I'm Brooklyn born-and-raised," Denim Debbie announced. "And I'm a gynecologist, if anyone needs a pap smear!"

Back in the courtroom, the judge welcomed us. She was salty and impressive. "Don't tweet," she said, taking her glasses off and rubbing her eyes. "Please don't tweet. If there's anything I can beg of you in this process, it's that. Can you promise not to?"

We nodded.

"You can tweet after," she said. "That's *my* promise to *you*." She put her glasses back on. "So—let's get you out of here by Christmas."

It was November thirteenth.

Day One

The early morning subway was jam-packed, it being rush hour and all—something I never experience as a member of the theater industry, where we roll in physically at noon and emotionally at three. The security line at the courthouse was a mob scene. "I'm a seated juror," I told the guard, and he nodded and escorted me through the crowd to the front.

"Make way," the guard said. "He's a seated juror."

A murmur of acknowledgment went through the crowd, and I puffed up a bit, drunk on attention, until I glanced back at the line and saw horror on everyone else's faces—*If I'm not careful today*, they were thinking, *I could end up like him.*

Denim Debbie was already holding court in the jury room. "I walked here from Grand Central," she was saying. "I don't like the crowds on the subway! They make me nervous! So me? I just walk. It's brisk, it's good."

I took a seat at the table. Other jurors filed in. There was polite chatter and the sharing of morning papers, and spirits in general seemed higher. I began compiling mental notes in an effort to keep track of everyone:

Juror #1: Korean female, real estate agent, claims she was first woman on OkCupid

Juror #2: Hispanic female, religious nut, keeps saying "the Lord willing"

Juror #3: Caucasian female, Sabbath observer, mother of two, eats bagels audibly but really nice

Juror #4: African-American male, older, stately, runs a boxing gym for at-risk youth, doesn't say much but has kind eyes

Juror #5: Chinese female, young, attending business school, also doesn't say much but does not have kind eyes

Juror #6: Caucasian female, recently retired from advertising, a narcoleptic and casual snob

Juror #7: Caucasian male, gay, writing this book

Juror #8: Caucasian male, retired contractor, crossword enthusiast and casual sexist

Juror #9: Caucasian male, mild-mannered IT guy, father of three and avid fan of *Doctor Who*

Juror #10: Caucasian female, older, elegant, always wrapped in a pashmina

Juror #11: Hispanic male, hospital administrator, talks nonstop about how much work he's missing

Juror #12: The worst

"Good morning," the judge said as we filed into the jury box. "Did you tweet? Good. Don't."

Opening arguments commenced. Ours was a drugs and guns case, with some possession and conspiracy charges. The hundred-and-fifty-year-old defense attorney, apparently exhumed just for the occasion, slowly rose and set out for the podium. Like the early settlers on the Oregon Trail, he reached his destination, but not without some losses along the way. He opened his manila folder and a bunch of neon Post-its promptly fell out and spilled all over the floor. The second- and third-chair attorneys ran to pick them up and tried to salvage the order, but it was officially fucked, and as a result his opening argument was a real hodgepodge:

"My client's never been to Bay Ridge," he read off of one Post-it, and then picked up a second and added, "A gun? He didn't have a gun. What he did have was a record label." From a third, he read, "And this business about a lease. We'll get to the lease."

Juror #6 promptly fell asleep, and her glasses fell off her head. The clerk gestured for me to wake her up. I tapped her shoulder, and she jumped as though I'd Tasered her. The judge glared at us. I turned bright red, mortified and furious at Juror #6 for getting me in trouble with a federal judge, even though guilt by association shouldn't hold up in a court of law!

"I know we aren't supposed to talk about the case," Denim Debbie started.

"We aren't," Juror #5 interjected.

"But did you see the prosecutor girl laughing during the old guy's opening argument?"

"We aren't supposed to talk about the . . ."

"I know," Denim Debbie continued, "but she's pretty and blond and probably went to some fancy school, so she thinks she's above him somehow. You still owe people respect."

Juror #5 tried again. "We really shouldn't talk about this yet."

"I know. It just irked me. It won't affect my judgment or anything."

Day Two

A wake-and-baker stunk up the train the whole way downtown. Juror #6 was twenty minutes late, probably fucking asleep in her doorway, and we all had to wait. "I'm sorry, I tried to call," she said as she sauntered in. "Luckily, I live only a few blocks away."

The prosecution showed us an array of scary guns, disposable cell phones, and drug-packaging materials, and I tried to eye them all prudently, as if I were on *Antiques Roadshow*. One of the prosecutors broke into a full sweat while trying to lug a kilo press over to the jury box. "Good thing my name's Samson," he quipped, and the "Lord Willing" Lady laughed appreciatively.

"Cut the theatrics," the judge interrupted. "The jury can see the kilo press perfectly well from where it is; it's enormous. Is it heavy?"

"Yes," Samson replied.

She turned to the court reporter and said, "Let the record reflect that the kilo press is heavy."

"I wouldn't want to be *her* husband," the Retired Contractor kept saying to every man in the room.

"No, siree," agreed the Hospital Administrator with a belly laugh.

I exchanged a look with the Sabbath Observer: they would be so *lucky* to be her husband.

Day Three

"Want a pepper?" Denim Debbie asked each of us as we walked into the jury room. "Want a pepper?" She had a Ziploc bag full of them. "I have to keep eating, for my metabolism. All this sitting! I'm gonna get so fat!" She cracked open a Diet Sprite. "All that's missing is my Stoli!" She pulled a straw from her purse and stuck it into the can. "My husband showed me an article about how you shouldn't put your mouth on cans."

That day, the prosecution hauled out enough cocaine to

fill an old town well, sealed in various quart-sized Ziploc bags, seized from the defendant's alleged stash house. The second chair from the defense stopped in the middle of a redirect on a witness to ask, "I'm sorry, Your Honor, but is the cocaine still in the courtroom?"

"Yes," the judge replied.

"Well, I'd like to make a motion that we remove it."

"Why?"

"Well, Your Honor, I'm a little embarrassed to admit this," he replied, lifting his shoulders and laughing a little, "but I'm starting to feel affected by it!"

She stared at him for a long, withering beat and then replied, "The cocaine stays. Enough with the 'moments.' Act like a lawyer."

"They should let us sample the evidence," the Retired Contractor kept saying on the next break. "Let us sample it, make sure it's real."

The First Woman on OkCupid cracked her neck and said, "No joke. I'm going to *need* some of it to get through this fucking trial."

Day Four

"Oh, Barbra Streisand," Denim Debbie said, slurping on a halved grapefruit and reading the headline of an article over someone's shoulder. "Shut up and sing, that's what I say. I liked her back when she was about the music. And I say this for people on both sides. Shut up and sing: no one wants to hear all of your opinions."

"Kidney stones?" she said later, picking up on someone's conversation from across the room. "You gotta zap 'em. Get in there and zap 'em. Oh, they're hell if you don't zap 'em."

"I had a pet snake," she told the room even later. "I used to let him slither all over me while I watched TV." I tried to imagine her at home, working out and watching *The Real Housewives*, covered in big snakes.

We heard testimony from a cagey biologist and a grizzled trap specialist.

"Can you list some of the items you've found hidden in traps in suspects' vehicles?" the blond prosecutor asked.

"Controlled substances, large quantities of cash, firearms," the trap specialist rattled off. "And also compact discs, photo albums, and, once, a ladies' personal massager."

"I've got to get me a trap!" Denim Debbie hooted back in the jury room.

Day Five

We were treated to testimony from an all-star lineup of charismatic cocaine dealers who've been in the *Post*. They were a hit. They were gifted storytellers, enthralling us with tales of standoffs at the Apollo and Bentley chases up the FDR, and they brandished so many bon mots along the way that I had to start writing them down. Did you know that two parallel ordeals are a "Kit Kat situation," or that if someone can be easily shot without witnesses, they are "gift-wrapped"?

On a break, Pashmina Lady leaned her elbows on the table and ran her hands through her hair. "How long is this going to drag on?" she moaned. "My life has just been turned upside down by this."

She opened a yogurt and began to eat it with a knife.

"You want a spoon?" one of the alternates asked.

"No, I always eat yogurt with a knife," she said.

Day Six

The prosecution called a handsome DEA agent as their final witness, and I perked up considerably. He strode to the witness stand, unbuttoned his suit jacket, and sat. He said hello to the court reporter and helped himself to the coffee provided. He'd done this before.

He looked like he would accept pie from the old ladies he questioned. He had British television eyes—melancholy, I assume, from all that he has seen. He ended a sentence with "and me," and then interrupted the prosecution to say, "Sorry, and *I.*"

May the record reflect the ringing of bells.

No further questions? Juror #7 has a few: *You like jazz? Why the DEA? Do you think the Oscars have gotten too irreverent?* It was clear why they called him last; he was a genetic mic drop. *Make of my body a house you suspect to contain drugs.*

"I miss the drug dealers," the Sleepy Snob said back in the jury room. "Those were good stories."

"I know," Pashmina Lady agreed. "Today is so boring."

"I don't know," I chimed in, "I liked that DEA agent; he seemed really funny and nice, like he's good at his job."

The room got quiet, and the First Woman on OkCupid shot me a look: *Dial it down.*

Day Seven

"All right," the judge said to us, "you've heard closing statements from both the prosecution and the defense, and now it's time for you to start to make some decisions about what you heard. Talk to each other, ask to see evidence again, keep an open mind. Just. Don't. Tweet."

Denim Debbie sat at the head of the table and opened up another Ziploc bag. "I don't think they have enough evidence," she said, her mouth full of fucking jicama. "Show me the fingerprints. Why didn't they get any fingerprints?"

The Mild-Mannered IT Guy snapped and said, "Because this isn't an episode of *Bones*."

Denim Debbie reared up, slapped her hand on the table, and shouted, "I don't WATCH *Bones!*"

"I don't think they proved their case," Juror #6 said haughtily. I turned to gape at her. She'd been in deep REM for half the trial; of course she wasn't convinced.

To my further shock, most of the people at the table nodded in agreement.

"I think those drug dealers were lying," the First Woman on OkCupid said.

"They're under oath," I said.

"Right," the Sabbath Observer agreed. "Even if they are lying, we have to assume they're being truthful."

"They'll say anything to get out of jail," Pashmina Lady interjected. "It happens all the time."

I couldn't believe what I was hearing. Were we all watching the same trial for the last seven days?

"And don't get me started on that lease," Denim Debbie said. "That lease did *not* look real."

The Sabbath Observer put her head in her hands. "If it wasn't real, it wouldn't have been admitted as evidence," she moaned.

"I don't know, it looked pretty fishy to me," Denim Debbie continued. "I agree, I don't think they proved their case. They were so cocky, laughing at the old guy, and yet they didn't prove it. Innocent until proven guilty!"

Over half the people at the table were sitting with their arms firmly folded, their lips pursed, shaking their heads—impenetrable. After six hours of deliberation, the four of us who thought the defendant was guilty caved. The opposing eight never wavered even slightly. I suppose it is crucial to some people that they be right, or, more importantly, that they have been right all along.

As we waited to go back into the courtroom, Denim Debbie's voice caught in her throat. "I'm really going to miss you guys," she said, and tears streamed down her cheeks. It was awkward. No one said anything back, but I looked at her, stunned. This was huge for her, I suddenly realized. Her husband gives her all her news. When was the last time something was her call?

I rode in the elevator with the Sabbath Observer and the Stately Boxing Ring Owner. "Better to let a maybe-guilty man go free than send an innocent one to jail," the Sabbath Observer said.

"What I don't understand," the Stately Boxing Ring Owner, who'd been silent throughout most of the trial, added, "is why these kids don't see it's not really *that* much harder to apply themselves, to go to business school and get a real degree and a real job. They're brilliant, and they could be running a real business. Such a goddamned waste, such a . . ." He stopped and looked at the elevator floor, shaking his head.

On the street we turned to each other and were all kind of

like, "Well, good-bye." I mean, there was no other word for what we were doing—we were saying good-bye, and one by one we each stepped into the commuter current and disappeared.

I turned thirty during the trial, and you haven't lived until you've had thirteen total strangers sing the first half of "Happy Birthday" to you, petering out one by one as they near that penultimate phrase and realize that they don't know your name.

Subway Diary

———

A train, 2:30 a.m., Saturday

"This is Seventy-Second Street; next stop Eighty-First," the conductor announces, his voice as sleepy as ours. "Stand clear of the closing doors."

The doors do not close.

"Excuse me, sir," the conductor suddenly says over the loudspeaker. "Please pick up that garbage you just threw onto the platform."

A moment.

"Yes, sir, you. In the hat. The one sticking your head out. I'm looking at you. See me? Hi."

Titters. People begin to stand and peer out of the car onto the platform.

"Please pick up your trash and put it in the garbage can," the conductor says calmly. "There's one a few steps down the platform. We'll wait for you."

We all begin to laugh a bit. A woman peeks her head out and reports to the man across from her, "He's down a few cars. He's doing it."

"There you go!" the conductor says after a moment. "You

picked up the trash. Now take it to the garbage can. We're all waiting on you, buddy. People want to get home."

There are hoots and hollers from the other cars.

"*Thank* you," the conductor continues. "You don't see me going to your place of work and throwing my trash around. I gotta be down here all day. It's just common courtesy. Stand clear of the closing doors, please; Eighty-First Street is next."

The doors close, and the train continues north. Everybody's laughing and clapping a little.

The loudspeaker crackles, and the conductor is back again. "Seriously, I don't understand some of you," he announces. "You bring that trash down here with you, you can take it out with you, too. You leave your food, your bottles, your garbage on all of the trains, and then you have the *nerve* to complain that the trains are dirty."

"Fuck!" the woman across from me shouts, "Now we *all* in trouble!"

D train, 9:30 p.m., Tuesday

A charming middle-aged man and his older female coworker have a funny conversation, both of them quick wits in suits. A young woman with a stroller gets on the train at Fifty-Ninth Street, and the man offers her his seat. She accepts, and as he stands nearby he makes faces at and talks with her toddler son in the stroller. The mother smiles, leans forward, and encourages her son to respond.

Behind the mother's back the man's coworker mouths, "*Talk to her! Talk to her! Talk! To! Her!*" and cocks her head toward the yes-very-beautiful young mother. The man repeatedly shakes his head. From my seat across from them I also want to mouth to him, "*Talk to her!*"

His coworker mouths it a few more times, until he shoots her a burning, halting look. She stops, locks her mouth with an imaginary key, and joins him in looking at the subway floor. Not even the kid can get the man's attention, and after a while his mother gets out a Ziploc bag of Cheerios for him, and that's the end of it.

A train, 5:30 p.m., Sunday

An older woman with groceries asks a beautiful young man with an accent—Caribbean, maybe—how long he's been in America.

"Two months," he tells her.

"How do your parents feel about you coming here?" she asks.

"My mother loves it," he says, "but my father says I'm like a girl." He's a model, it turns out, which has brought great shame to his father. "But he says, if you're going to have picture taken, send money home, take care of your family who took care of you."

"And are you taking care of yourself?" the older woman asks. "Are you staying away from drugs?"

"I go to parties," he answers. "I have to, to get my name out there, to get publicity."

The older woman shakes her head. "You cannot be doing those drugs," she says. "You have to get rest and you have to eat right, or else everything you have will go."

He tells her about a party he was at just the night before, at the house of a designer who was premiering a new line. "There was this big bowl of coke in the middle of the room, and people were scooping out of it all night," he says.

The older woman shakes her head again. "Oh, no," she murmurs, "no, no, no. Did you do it?"

"I had to," he replies. "He said I looked like I wasn't having any fun. He wants me to wear his clothes."

"You need to make sure you are making good choices," she says. "Make your mother proud."

The train pulls into the Fifty-Ninth Street station. He looks out the window, then leans forward in his seat.

"Do you know where you are going?" the older woman asks him.

"Upstairs?" he asks.

She nods. "Take the 1 train to Seventy-Second Street and transfer to the 2. It's a straight shot from there." He stands up, and she adds, "You know, when you got on the train, I could see in you that you'll be a star. You have that energy."

He beams. "I am," he says. "You're going to see me in magazines."

She takes his hand. "Stay healthy and safe. This country is beautiful, and this country is toxic. Your mother loves you, so keep that close to you. You hear?"

He leans in, kisses her on the cheek and says good-bye, and is gone.

The Dark Place

No matter where you are, you're never far from the Dark Place. It's a late-night malaise. Portals include bars, family reunions, odd-numbered seating arrangements where you're at the end of the table like an extremity, jokes you missed the beginning of, sing-alongs, and Playbill.com. Like catching the train to Hogwarts from Platform 9 and 3/4, you, too, are whisked away into a magical world unseen by the general public. Through the train window you can see the bridge you just crossed blow up and crumble into the river below.

In the Dark Place Welcome Center, Bonnie Raitt and Morrissey, the Poet Laureates, sing from Bose speakers tastefully hidden in planters and behind rocks. Help yourself to the complimentary rose-tinted glasses in the bins by the exits. There are weeping willows to sit under. The café menu boasts warm humble pie and local foot in mouth. Then, the thoughts arrive:

You don't have as much of a way with children as you think you do
You don't have as much of a way with adults as you think you do

Everyone at this party could take you or leave you
Your mouth is less of a sex organ and more of a veterans' hospital
Everything ends
You have a FUPA

In terms of how to find your way out of the Dark Place, here's the route I've found most successful: Go home, sit on your couch, and watch one episode of *Roseanne*. Go to sleep. You'll feel better in the morning. And if you don't, they made eight seasons of *Roseanne*. Well, nine, although I don't count that batshit-crazy last one.

Where Is Your Shakespeare?

- - - - - - -

I do have a favorite customer. She's an old woman who wears a beret and has a vague, mannered accent. "Where is your Shakespeare?" she's always asking. "Do you have any Shakespeare for me?"

I tell her the price, and without fail she'll slam her hand on the windowsill and say, "What is this, air travel?!"

One time she came by and there was a gritty prison drama loading into the theater, so a lot of set pieces were in the lobby. "There is a toilet in your hallway," she said to me. "This cannot be Shakespeare." I told her a little bit about the show, to which she replied, "Oh, can't you offer me something more cheerful?"

"You think Shakespeare is cheerful?" I asked, and she said, "When someone dies that beautifully, yes."

Another time she asked me if I'd seen the play she was buying tickets to, and when I said no, that it was hard for me to commit to an additional three hours at work most nights, she told me that if I continued my life in such a way, I would come to regret it. "You have three hours you can give to Shakespeare," she said.

It turns out she lives in my neighborhood, or, I should say, I live in *her* neighborhood. "Hey neighbor," I said, "I'm on 181st," and she declared, "You are below the Spanish steps. I call them that because they have grand steps just like that in Rome. Have you been to Rome?"

I told her no, and she said, "Let me guess. It's hard for you to commit to it."

"There are other factors, too!" I protested, but she *tsk-tsk*ed, tucked her ticket envelope into her wallet, grabbed her cane, and said, "You are young, and you are rich with time. People who desire money can have it. I desire time."

Love Poem for the
Classiest Gay Guy on Avenue A

I'm sitting in a bar
at a party for a friend,
trying on a brown liquor evening for size.
I see you outside on the street corner;
both of you are framed nicely by the window I'm sitting at,
you and your friend.
His head is pressed to yours,
snowflakes are salt-and-peppering the air around you,
and I think to myself,
All right, I'll watch them make out a little;
it'll kill time while the ice melts and appeases this
sulfuric acid in my glass.

But then his arms drop from around you
to dangle at his side,
and he pitches forward a little,
and it becomes clear that you are supporting all of his weight.
You embrace him not as lover

but as buttress,

and without you standing there

he would surely drop to the ground like a sack of potatoes,

like the sack of potatoes that made the vodka

I could've ordered, but no, I wanted to be like

Glenn Close on *Damages*.

He is very drunk.

Your hands go to either side of his face

and you speak directly to him

with loving firmness.

You reach for something in his pockets,

and he squirms, dodges you,

runs from you,

all with his head still pressed to yours.

It's like you're a maypole

and he's a ribbon that won't remember any of this in the morning.

Finally you procure a phone from his pocket,

and as you dial a number he pushes away from you

and stumbles jelly-legged into traffic.

You pull him back and hold him

by the nape of the neck

with one hand,

and again you speak to him with that

loving firmness,

and oh, how I'd love for you to speak to me that way

in Duane Reade

or when I can't pick a restaurant.

My drink diluted a little,
I swish a sip around and down and
ache to be yours.
It tastes like the holidays we could share,
our families.

I imagine you're calling your friend's roommate,
making sure she'll be up to help him out of the cab
and up the stairs and into bed.
And to call you once he's there,
lest you start to worry.
My god, you're the most wonderful person
I've never met.

You put his phone back in his pocket
and turn to hail a cab,
your charcoal coat open,
the crisp white shirt you're wearing the fuck out of underneath
hardly protecting you from the elements.
Who, I nearly wonder aloud, do you have to
remind you to button your coat,
especially on Avenue A,
where people give each other piggyback rides
and hepatitis C?

I want to put on lipstick
and kiss all the collars of your shirts.
I wanted this to be my Year of Yes
but I just keep digging in my heels on every little thing.

Whitney Houston died today;
I remember making carpet angels
on my bedroom floor when I was eleven
and listening to the *Bodyguard* cassette tape
over and over again,
and OH, THERE'S THE BROWN LIQUOR.

Funny, with vodka it's quips and doom,
but with these burning brown sips
all I want to do is run my bare boy-feet through that carpet
and tell my parents I love them
without being all awkward about it,
and feel your hand on the back of my neck when the fan collects
those first flecks of shit, I swear to god,
I'm scared of so many simple, inevitable things.

I am also suddenly in the mood for hard-won accordion music.

I look up and you both are gone.
Perhaps you got into the cab, too;
perhaps you thought you'd have better luck one block west
(you will);
perhaps you put him in a cab as planned and walked off,
coat and shirt open to the flurries,
to continue your night.

The Rural Northwestern
Ohio Tragedy Tour

- - - - - - -

M y parents, my brother, and I were driving around with my grandmother in Ohio over the holiday. Hers being a town of staggering smallness, she knew the inhabitants of every house we passed. Invariably something horrible had happened to all of them. In that house on the right lived a couple who threw a barbecue one summer; their sons got too close to the fire, and the fire "got the boys." Just down that road a ways was a young woman from Mexico who gave up everything she knew to live on her new husband's farm; his tractor flipped over on him in a ditch. Next cornfield over belonged to a newly retired couple who were trying to be more active in their third act; on one of the morning walks they were really starting to love they were mowed down by three bicyclists from out of town who didn't slow on their turns and didn't see them, you know, over the corn.

We began to dread every new story. It was a census of fatal mishaps. My grandmother's eyes would catch sight of a house in the lessening distance, and she'd say, "Oh, you know who lives in that house? Ralph Lerner, from church," and after a while we'd all shout, "No! Stop! Don't tell us anything else about Ralph Lerner; we don't want to get attached or start to care about him!"

Later in the trip, my grandmother said to me, "I never wanted to marry your grandfather, you know." I was standing in her doorway, and we'd been talking about New York. She continued, "I wanted to move to the city and become a journalist. But Grandpa's love was like God's love. It took hold of me and my life." Another night we were dropping her off at her retirement home, and as she got out of the car, she said, "Sometimes I shake my fist up at heaven and I say, 'Darn you, Hal; you left me here!'"

She hugged my mother and said to her, "I'm ready to go. I'm just ready to go, you know?" and we walked her to her door. I didn't know what to say. I cannot imagine being ready to go. But there's time for that, I suppose. It's a life's work.

The Woodsman

- - - - - - -

How I came to be standing in a clearing in the middle of the woods in New Hampshire at four o'clock in the morning is rather simple: I was at an artists' colony, and I was looking for an artist with whom to colonize.

I was in the final days of a monthlong residency, tiptoeing through the very same woods Thornton Wilder, Aaron Copland, and Leonard Bernstein tiptoed through, but I was doing it at four in the morning, and I was doing it because of a boy. I could hear Willa Cather and Wendy Wasserstein hissing from the ether: *Slut*.

James Baldwin, on the other hand, was like: *Get it*.

I'd been wearing the same boots for twenty-nine days. I hadn't known precisely how to pack for a month away—and a month away in the woods, at that. What transitions ably from day to night, from cocktail party to bear attack? What could be easily pried from the talons of a goshawk, or someone who wants to talk about their agent? And, most importantly, what could project a rustic down-to-fuck energy should I need to summon some sartorially?

At any given time there would be twenty-five world-class artists around me, and I thought maybe I'd meet my husband, or at least make out with someone who'd been to the Sudan on a grant. So I packed nice underwear, my favorite cardigan, and two of every toiletry, a Neutrogena Noah's ark; the town for which I was headed inspired Grover's Corners and would most likely be well stocked with folksy profundities but not my Pantene Pro-V Women of Color conditioner.

The other residents were even more impressive than I'd hoped, and I immediately set out to scrutinize their friendly behavior for any signs of gay life—*his gait is a bit prissy, he really made a scrumptious meal out of that word, is that a cowl neck on that sweater?*—mating by McCarthyism. One after the other, they all turned out to be merely flamboyant, worldly straight men. They might've been gay in a moment that suited them artistically—"Because what is sexuality anyway," they might ask, "besides a gendered prison conjured up by the advertising industry?" to which I might respond, "Okay, I have a lot of layers on, and it's at least five minutes from here to naked, so get to the thesis—are we doing this or not?"

I positively ached for a photographer who was such an authority on his own work and soul that I nearly ate my hand. I played Ping-Pong with a Gyllenhaal-eyed architect who kept bringing up his wife, perhaps because I moaned throughout each volley. I talked for an hour about boats with a filmmaker who looked like Ronan Farrow, only to have him then talk about sailing in one of them to visit his girlfriend in Europe, with whom up until that point he'd had only an online relationship—you know, he might've been gay and just trying to fend me off.

My dream of being fisted by a MacArthur Genius threatened to be just that: a dream. I thought, *Maybe you should calm down and value this time. Everyone's here to be really serious and get serious work done. This isn't Club Med; this isn't twenty-eight Stellas concurrently getting their Grooves back*—but no, people fucked. Hands would linger on corduroyed knees around the fireplace. People started wearing lipstick to dinner. Those who were usually loud and boisterous were now quiet, listening attentively at someone's side. People who never came to breakfast would come to breakfast.

I gave up and told myself that if I was to gain anything from a month in the woods, I'd have to starve myself of the usual distractions—namely, Facebook, Twitter, and porn. I removed everything from my phone, reducing it to, well, a phone.

I sat day after day in my studio, staring alternately at the computer screen and out the window. I listened to entire albums. I dared myself to eat the piece of fruit that came with each lunch. I read about Ruth Bader Ginsburg. I masturbated in front of spiders. It snowed, and I watched it. I began unabashedly talking to myself, and talking to myself as if I were a child—"What do you want to do today?" "Before we leave, do you have everything?"— which quickly devolved into a passive-aggressive marriage with myself—"Do you want to maybe take your dishes to the sink?"

I waited for hours on the station platforms of my mind for trains of thought to pull in, but few did.

The solitude unnerved me. Without social media I felt like a tree falling unheard in the woods—was my life even happening with no one to Like it? I started taking walks around the colony grounds, which admittedly were stunning, and I had to leave my phone in my studio because the urge to photograph everything stunned me further. The experience has been replaced by the experience of people knowing we had the experience; the picture is now secondary to the frame.

Halfway through my residency an actual gay person arrived, and that night the sun set in deep mauves in celebration. I stared at his back during dinner—he was broad, femmy, and lean. A short-story writer from Miami, he had arms that clanged with bracelets, eyes that wintered behind dark sunglasses, and a neck that hosted a symposium of scarves. He rarely smiled. He knitted during people's readings and showings. He spoke in curt, up-talky half sentences: "My boyfriend is in advertising?" he asked-told me. "He works for a gossip magazine? It's called *People*?"

"I'm familiar with it," I replied.

"We're in an open relationship?" he asked-said, which, to be fair, is how I've heard anyone in that scenario say it.

I immediately wrote him off as affected and dull, and he didn't seem the least bit charmed by me, either. He would walk through the woods wearing tight pink pants and noise-canceling head-phones, edgy and serene, while I skittered along, sing-sobbing Sondheim and avoiding any and all low-hanging branches in case a deer tick was thirsty for type A-negative blood. That's not my blood type; I'm just Type-A, negative, and I have blood.

*   *   *

The woods do not have people or sounds in them. I have been told this is part of their appeal.

"All the New Yorkers freak out here," one of the groundskeepers told me. "One guy left after the first night, said he couldn't take it. Me? I couldn't take New York. I love it here. I garden naked here." She looked at me and softened a bit. "Go to the amphitheater. It's pretty. You'll like it."

I never got used to it. Each night after dinner I'd run down the snowy, muddy path back to my studio, which was tucked into a thicket of tall trees that looked like anorexic demon arms reaching up to strangle curious birds. The lights of my studio turned each window dark and opaque, and yet I knew from the outside I could be seen clearly. I would frantically draw each curtain, turn off every light, and lay awake, covers to chin.

Gone was the late-night noise of my neighborhood: the hiccupping pump of brakes from off-duty buses, the trash can lid being lifted in the alley, the shouted half sentences floating up from drunk people stumbling into the bodega for provisions. In its place was . . . silence. Silence, and only every now and then a whisper of wind, or the creak of an eave under the snow's weight, or—

This silence felt not like the absence but the presence of something. I felt seen. It was so quiet it felt loud, like that moment between a breath in and a breath out. The woods' lungs seemed full, as if they were ready at any moment to speak.

And then, finally, they did.

It was my final week at the colony, and my mother called to tell me that my grandmother had died. She told me to finish my residency, that the funeral would happen after. I didn't know what to do, so I went to find the amphitheater the grounds-keeper had spoken of. It was a fine morning. I trudged through knee- and sometimes waist-deep snow and sat on the hundred-year-old amphitheater steps and listened to the wind through the jack pine trees. I'd looked up their names to try to better relate to them, and, perhaps touched by my effort and of course already knowing of my loss, they stood in hardened sympathy.

If we have to go, I figured—*And we do have to go*, the jack pines suddenly hummed—we should all go like she did: quickly, with minimal pain and family close by. In her final days she'd started saying to every doctor, every nurse, every medical professional stopping in to see her, "My father was a doctor, my brother was a doctor, my husband was a doctor, and I wanted to be a doctor, too, but my father wouldn't let me." This was news to all of us, and she delivered it so matter-of-factly. She harbored no malice or self-pity—she merely wanted it to be known before she went. And now we knew, and now, if you'll forgive me, you know, too.

Three days before I left, the colony held its annual gala. Our seating assignments at dinner, we were told, were very deliberate, and I was seated directly behind a pole with the board members' wives. These regal older women and I took a moment to size each other up. They looked at me like they could see where all the dicks had been. We stuck to three safe areas of conversation: grandchildren, the salad, and Broadway.

"Have you seen *Kinky Boots*?" the impeccably pearled matron to my left asked.

"I haven't, no," I replied.

"It's . . . *different*," she said. "Fun, but . . . different."

Once the festivities were over, we residents continued to drink. The staff wheeled out cases of extra booze. We'd been drinking cheap wine and Campari for the last month, so we ran for the Belvedere and Woodford Reserve like they were cookies on the moon. Music was turned on and up, and the freer spirits began to dance. One of the composers found me sitting off to the side and, top-shelf tipsy, slammed her hands down on the table and said, "If you do not sleep with him tonight, I am going to *kill you.*"

She pointed to the short-story writer, who was dancing in the center of the room. He'd pulled the bottom of his shirt up behind his head, exposing his torso, and he was all swiveling hips, undulating back, and liquid shoulders and arms.

"Sleep with him!" the composer shouted. "My ex is Latin; you will not regret it. I mean, I regret it, but you won't."

I looked around the table, and the memoirists and sculptors and silk-screeners were all in each other's arms and nodding *Do it.* As if on cue, the short-story writer came over, pulled down his shirt, and mopped his brow. "Hi," I said.

He turned to me, and in (as of this writing) the sexiest moment of my life, said, "Let's go home."

There was no question mark at the end of that sentence. It was a period.

"Let me see your studio," he said as we neared it, and, once inside, "Let's go to bed."

He removed his shirt and pants and reclined in jock-strapped repose. I stripped to my *Chicago: The Musical* nightshirt and underwear and slid in next to him. *At long last*, I thought, *my woodsy colony mate, my rustic fuck*. I nuzzled his shoulder, sparky and ignitable like the dry timber outside.

He looked at the ceiling. "I'm having a hard time with my story?" he suddenly asked-said.

"Oh?" I replied, sojourning a palm across his stomach. "What's it about?"

His jaw clicked. He was rotating it. "It's about a pedophile?" he finally asked-answered, and then asked-continued, "It's about my dad?"

I slowly withdrew my hands from his body. "What?"

As if he were a glass of bourbon knocked over at the benefit, the whole awful story spilled out of him, and I did my best to keep it from running off the bed. I couldn't believe he was telling it to me. "Holy shit," I kept saying. "I'm sorry, holy shit." The air around us felt electric, the way it can when you're close to real horror. My eyes darted to the window, and outside stood the trees, a rapt Greek chorus. *The world can be horrible*, they hummed. *You cannot make sense of it; you can only absorb it.*

"Let's go to sleep?" he asked-said.

I turned off the light, and in the dark he pulled me to him. I was hard. I had been hard the whole walk there, and drunk, he was drunk, we were both drunk, and the thought knocked at the screen door at the back of my mind: *Do you think we'll still hook up?*

I put both my hands to his chest. His body was warm, and it was a small bed. I found his mouth with mine and we kissed.

"Turn over," he said.

I did as he said, and he draped his arm around me and again

pulled me close. He smelled like musk and dancing to Beyoncé, and his jock-strapped cock pressed squarely against my ass. I ground against it, hoping to rouse him.

"It's so nice to have somebody to cuddle with," he said, suddenly. "The nights are so lonely."

"Mm, yeah," I mumbled, putting a stop to the grinding and trying to keep up. I looked around the room and realized that, with him there, it was the first time I'd been in this bed and not scared. "I know; I've been so, like, freaked out each night," I said, taking his hand in mine. "I think my studio might be haunted or something."

"Also, the pickings are so slim on Grindr," he added.

My eyes flipped open bitterly in the dark, like two balls of white in the solid black panel of a cartoon strip called *Are You Fucking Kidding Me?* He quickly fell asleep and began to snore bourbon CO_2 into my ear. And like that we lay, two spooning slim pickings, until morning.

Two afternoons later I woke from a nap to find him standing at my door. Colonists are not allowed to approach each other's studios unless invited, like vampires, but I find blatant misconduct titillating, so I sat up and said, "Hey."

He held a bag from the stationery store in town and a bouquet of fresh flowers from the place with the twenty-dollar jams. "I thought we could go to my studio and read together?" he asked-said.

Our boots crunched in the snow underfoot on the way to his studio, which overlooked a grand meadow. Inside there were huge windows from which you could gaze out at it. "There's always deer and shit," he said. He made tea in his electric kettle, and we sat by the fireplace. He lit a cigarette.

"You can't smoke in here!" I said, officially the home-schooled girl at the sleepover.

He shrugged and blew smoke at the ceiling. "What's your type?" he suddenly asked, looking up from his book.

"What do you mean?"

"You know, what's your type? Who's your ideal man?"

"I don't know," I said. "Matt Damon?"

"Matt Damon's an idiot," he said. He stood, stretched, and stripped off his shirt and pants. Again he stood in front of me in his jockstrap. My jaw dropped. "I'm going to take a shower before dinner," he said. "You're welcome to stay, if you want." He closed the bathroom door behind him.

"Um, I think I'll just see you at dinner," I called through the door.

"Okay," he replied, already in the shower.

I grabbed my book, which ironically was *The Sense of an Ending*, something I've never had, and left. *What the fuck?* I thought on the walk back to my studio. *Why am I only able to assert myself sexually with strangers?* I paused on the path. The trees kept mum.

On the last night of my residency I texted him: "Want to come over?"

He texted back: "I've already brushed my teeth and I'm naked. Want to come here?"

Well, that seemed pretty clear!

And so there I was, at four in the morning, marching fearlessly through the woods, impervious to the snaps of branches and hoots of owls that had previously tortured me. He answered the door in his jockstrap, an article of clothing I now felt stood between us like a competitive, possessive child from his previous marriage. I resented it.

"Hi," I said.

"I thought we could watch a movie," he replied.

I followed him to his bed, in front of which he'd queued up *Dangerous Liaisons* on one of the colony's televisions. He slid into bed. I stripped to my underwear and climbed in next to him. He handed me the remote. "In case I fall asleep and you want to turn it off," he said.

We started to watch the movie. *Put that remote on the night table and grab something else!* I screamed internally at myself.

He yawned.

He's yawning, *you idiot—do something: put a hand on his stomach, put your head on his shoulder, lean in and kiss him!*

I stared at the screen, watching Glenn Close conspire with John Malkovich, and felt my heart race.

Reach for him!

I couldn't. I turned off the movie and the lights and flopped down in the bed next to him. He rolled over, his back now to me. What had he wanted from me? Certainly not sex. He was a gorgeous, talented writer; I'm sure he had plenty of sex. Maybe what he did not have plenty of were people to confide in, people to feel close to. Could it have been that he felt close to me?

I sat up and looked out at the meadow. Thunder rumbled in the distance.

Finally, on the station platform of my mind a lone train rolled in, a cargo train carrying the memory of my first time, and I boarded it. At a sleepover at his mother's house, my very first boyfriend and I undressed and fumbled through what felt like a checklist of steps, as if a lost virginity were a piece of Ikea furniture we were assembling together. He put Vaseline on the condom and was painfully inside of me for no more than thirty seconds when he ran out of the room and vomited in the hallway. I lay there, startled and confused, while he cleaned it and himself up. When he came back into the room, he sat on the bed and told me he was having flashbacks to being molested as a child and couldn't continue, nor could he be near me. He slept on the bed and I slept on the floor. I broke up with him the next day, and for years after I resented him deeply, not really considering or grappling with the immensity of his hurt. He has since moved on and found happiness and peace, and lovers. "I'm truly sorry you can't do the same," he said to me in an instant-message fight I started with him years later.

I looked at the writer next to me.

Reach for him.

I shook my head. He'd wanted to feel closer to someone through not-sex for once, and I couldn't take away his hurt, but I could at least give him that. Hopefully there would be others to try to reach for in the night.

I found my shirt and my pants and my socks and my shoes. I took one last look at him, sleeping, a moonlit statue of a man, and left. Out in the clearing there was an ethereal brightness, a lustrous mist all around. My footsteps could not have made a sound if I'd tried. A skunk materialized ahead of me on the path, and we both stopped and stared at each other. An armistice. Finally it continued on, and a moment later so did I. The trees, who had earlier hummed *The world can be horrible. You cannot make sense of it; you can only absorb it*, now continued, *But if you try like we do, your exhale can be cleaner than your inhale.*

And back to my studio I went, to be by myself in the woods, to be myself in the woods, and to ride out another night.

Love Poem for the Couple in the Honeymoon Stage across from Me on the Subway

- - - - - - -

My first instinct was to mock them,
which I suppose reveals something about me.

It's just that they were sitting there
in their summer shirts and winter scarves
clinging to each other in the middle of the day,
and what was I to do?

She held a book with both hands, down low—
I couldn't make out the title—
but on its way to the book her right arm rested on his left,
and he in turn held his book—
Blood Meridian—
with his left hand,
and with his right he gripped the crook of her arm
gently, faux-inconsequentially.

They were sweet.
They were so young.
They were so still.

They did not look at each other, not even once.
They didn't move.
They just read.

Or did they?
The train rumbled farther and farther downtown—
116th Street, 103rd Street, 96th, 86th, 72nd—
and neither of them turned a page.

Maybe they struggled with reading.
Maybe that's how they met.

Or maybe, I suddenly thought, they feared turning the page.

They would have to move—
she would have to withdraw her arm,
and he would have to lift his hand.
Funny how the ceasing calls more attention
to the act than the act itself,
but then they would no longer not have held each other on
the subway like that before,
in the middle of the day, with books,
and she would not have never before shyly angled her body
toward him in public,

nor would his thumb have never before made gentle wind-
shield-wipes on her arm.

Will it ever be this new again,
this simple?

Two cells in the bloodstream of a city.

They don't turn the page,
and I don't blame them.

I've been reading the same one for years.

Acknowledgments

I am greatly indebted to many for their help and support along the way:

To the wonderful people at Ars Nova, The MacDowell Colony, SPACE on Ryder Farm, Vineyard Arts Project, the Belle Foundation, and The New 42nd Street.

To my editor, John Glynn, and everyone at Scribner; to Spencer Kimble for the cover; to my agent, Ross Harris, for flexing his muscles and making it all happen; to Jocelyn Florence and Kelsey Smith for the jump start; and to Polly Hubbard and Peter Hagan for the early direction.

To Di Glazer, Daniel Loeser, Ian Cheney, Michele Chadwick, Cristina Sanza, Colin Hanlon, Matthew-Lee Erlbach, Matt Cleaver, Jack Lienke, Courtney Caldwell, Amanda Duarte, John Early, Kevin Cahoon, Heather Levine, Cory Michael Smith, Ben Rimalower, Will Sherrod, and Anne Ray for their eyes, their ears, and, often, their shoulders.

To Aryn Kyle and Tim Federle for their generosity and good counsel.

To my brother, Nathan, for dressing up with me then and putting up with me now.

To David Ruttura, Micah Bucey, Melanie Hopkins, Ian McWethy, Carrie McCrossen, and Bear Mansfield, who read and listened to these stories at every step of the way and answered every flare sent up in the night.

And, lastly, to Jason Eagan, for his guidance, his friendship, and his calm California confidence, without which I never would've had the courage.

Thank you all.

About the Author

- - - - - - -

Isaac Oliver is a playwright, author, and performer. His stories have been featured in the How I Learned Series, the Soundtrack Series, *Showgasm*, *Dead Darlings*, *Real Characters*, *On This Island*, and *Naked Radio*. He lives in New York City.